ONE DISH FISH

ONE DISH FISH

70 QUICK & SIMPLE RECIPES
TO COOK IN THE OVEN

Lola Milne

Photography by Lizzie Mayson

Kyle Books

CONTENTS

INTRODUCTION

Seafood and fish seem to strike fear into the hearts of many, even those who are fairly confident in the kitchen, but this really needn't be the case. *One Dish Fish* will show you how to cook fish and how to do so well, without any faffing or fiddle – and all within one dish. The book is centred around the versatile roasting tin. It's perfect for low-maintenance suppers: simply pop the ingredients in and – with perhaps just a bit of stirring and sprinkling – *voilà*, out comes a full meal.

One Dish Fish will help you gain confidence when cooking fish and seafood and provide you with some basic guidance on seasonality, sustainability and fish types. Each recipe has flexibility built in, allowing you to tailor it to the time of year or what you have available; within most recipes, there are alternative fish suggested. I have largely tried to steer clear of overly expensive ingredients, as fish is on the dearer side as it is. I've also tried to avoid those fish that are, across the board, hugely on the decline; however, this isn't very clear-cut, as fish stocks differ greatly from area to area, so you may want to do a little research into the situation in your region. Let's try to be conscientious fish eaters!

This book is predominantly pescatarian, but not exclusively; perhaps this is not what you expect. Meat and fish can be delicious together; meat can complement and elevate fish, contributing extra layers of flavour. I am keen to push eating less meat, but I do not personally cut it out entirely. The recipes in this book that use meat do so sparingly, and there are alternative options to make it work without, if you prefer.

Fish and seafood can be wonderfully quick to prepare and cook, not to mention delicious and nutritious. This book is geared towards helping you make the most of this speed and convenience, with most dishes ready within 30 minutes. You won't find super-long ingredients lists or lengthy methods; these are recipes that can be made by anyone, in almost any size of kitchen, well equipped or otherwise (as long as you have an oven!).

The chapters are divided by time frame: 20 minutes, 30 minutes and 45 minutes. Whether you have very limited time or slightly longer, there are recipes to suit you: simple tray bakes, delicious pastas, hearty stews or warm salads – all made in a roasting tin. Here you'll find countless options for weekday dinners and light lunches, as well as dishes for when you want to show off a little at the weekend. I aim to arm you with an array of quick and easy fish-based meals, so that you can get as much joy as possible out of cooking and eating fish.

A NOTE ABOUT OVENS

All oven temperatures given in this book are for conventional ovens. If you are cooking in a fan oven, follow the manufacturer's instructions for adjusting the time and the temperature.

All ovens are different. Consider the cooking times in the recipes as a guide, not a scripture. Get to know your oven: does it, on the whole, cook things faster than recipes say? Is there one side of the oven that seems to cook things quicker than the other? How long does it take to preheat? It is worth investing in an oven thermometer if you suspect something is a little funky. Most importantly, check your food and judge whether it is ready based on the visual cues in the recipes and my tips for checking whether fish is cooked on page 11. Try not to let out of sight mean out of mind: just because it's in the oven, don't think it doesn't need monitoring.

A NOTE ON ROASTING TINS

Each recipe in the book has a recommended tin size. I've stuck to four rough sizes to make life simpler and less cluttered.

EXTRA SMALL: 23cm (9in) long, 17cm (6½in) wide, 6cm (2½in) deep

SMALL: 30cm (12in) long, 17–18cm (6½–7in) wide, 6cm (2½in) deep

MEDIUM: 32cm (12½in) long, 20cm (8in) wide, 7cm (2¾in) deep

LARGE: 34cm (13½in) long, 24cm (9½in) wide, 7cm (2¾in) deep

I prefer using a heavy metal or non-stick roasting tin for the recipes in this book, but you can use a Pyrex or ceramic dish. If you use a tin that differs significantly in size from that recommended in the recipe, the cooking times will need adjusting. In general, when you're roasting vegetables or fish, sizing up is better than sizing down – sizing down will result in a longer cooking time and potentially sweaty vegetables. When cooking recipes that involve an absorption method, such as the pasta- and rice-based dishes, do try to stick to the size of tin specified, as deviating could cause problems with the cooking time and effectiveness of the absorption. You don't want to end up with something too wet or dry.

NAVIGATING FISH

Welcome to this little overview on how to navigate the world of fish. I'm here to help you avoid the pitfalls or panic that – let's face it – cooking fish can sometimes induce.

MEET THE FISH

Let's start with the loose groups of fish that you commonly encounter: white fish, oily fish and shellfish. In the table below, you can see a selection of each.

WHITE FISH	OILY FISH	SHELLFISH
Cod	Mackerel	Clam
Dover sole	Sardine	Mussel
Hake	Trout	Prawn
Haddock	Salmon	Crab
Monkfish	Herring	Squid
Lemon sole	Anchovy	
Plaice	Tuna	
Pollock		
Pollack		
Sea bream		
Sea bass		
Tilapia		

I have tried to use a wide range of different (but accessible) fish and shellfish, and each recipe includes a list of good alternatives to aid you with any issues around availability or seasonality. If you use an alternative, bear in mind that the substitute fish may be thicker or thinner than the fish used in the recipe, and this will affect how quickly it cooks. If it's thinner, remember to keep an eye on it as it may cook sooner than the recipe says. If it's thicker, you may need to cook it for slightly longer. Using frozen fish and shellfish is absolutely fine; just make sure to defrost thoroughly before use. With fillets and whole fish, 24 hours in the refrigerator should do it. With prawns, I tend to submerge the bag in tepid water, which defrosts them very quickly.

PREPARATION AND CARE

If you're buying your fish from a supermarket pre-packaged, it should be fully prepared for you (scaled and, if whole, gutted). If you're buying it from the fish counter or a fishmonger, ask them to prepare it for you: you want it scaled, gutted and, if you're buying fillets, pin-boned. When you're buying squid that isn't pre-packaged, ask the fishmonger to clean, gut and remove the quill inside. You may still want to give it a little rinse before cooking it to get rid of any gritty bits left hanging around.

COOKING

When cooking fish, slightly undercooking is umpteen times better than overcooking. You can, after all, eat most fish raw, but there aren't any recipes calling for raw fish in this book. There are a number of ways to check whether fish is done:

- When cooking a whole fish, cutting two or three slashes down to the bone on the side facing up allows you to see the flesh more easily, therefore making checking for doneness more straightforward. Bear in mind that, if you do this in a recipe that doesn't specify it, you may need to slightly reduce the cooking time, as the slashes will also help the fish cook faster. It won't make a huge difference; just take a peek about 5 minutes earlier than you would have to see how it's getting on.

- When cooking a whole fish, give the skin a good prod with your finger: the flesh should feel firm below the skin. You can also investigate the fish with the point of a knife: the flesh should come away from the bones easily.

- When cooking fillets, look out for the flesh becoming opaque and flaking easily.

- Clams and mussels should pop open when they're cooked.

- Raw prawns should turn from grey to pink.

- Some people prefer to eat their salmon slightly rare; this is totally OK. If you want to eat the fish like this, just start checking on the salmon a little earlier than the timings specified in the recipe. The fish should still flake, but will look a little blushed in the centre.

SERVING

FILLETS

When it comes to serving fish, fillets are straightforward, as the work has been done for us. We just get to choose whether or not we eat the skin. I prefer a crispy skin, but some love it regardless.

WHOLE ROUND FISH

When serving a whole round fish (such as trout, sea bass, mackerel or bream), the easiest way to do this is as follows:

1 Pull away the fins from the top and bottom of the fish. Some small bones that are attached should come away.

2 Using a sharp knife, cut down vertically behind the back of its head, to separate the head from the fillet.

3 Cut along the top of the fish, along the backbone towards the tail.

4 Make a downward cut when you get to the tail end of the fillet to separate the fillet at that end, too.

5 Take a butter knife or spatula and carefully slip it underneath the fillet on the side facing you. Lift the fillet on to your plate.

6 Peel away the spine, starting at the tail end. It should come away fairly easily, including the head, but be sure to check for meat in the head before discarding it. You should now have two beautiful fillets to enjoy! (If your filleting all goes to pot, don't worry – just enjoy the fish, watching out for bones.)

WHOLE FLAT FISH

To serve a flat fish, the process isn't too dissimilar:

1 Lift the fish on to a plate or board, skin-side up. Score a line horizontally down the middle of the fish, along the spine, to divide the top two fillets.

2 Carefully run a butter knife under one of the fillets, lifting the flesh away from the bones. Allow the fillet to come away and set it down, skin-side down.

3 You'll see a fin running along the edge of the fillet rather like a wing: this contains lots of little bones. Gently pull it away and discard.

4 Repeat with the other top fillet.

5 Lift the spine from the tail end and peel away from the flesh. The head should come away, too.

6 You'll be left with the two bottom fillets. Again, pull away the wing-like fins. You should now have a deboned flat fish!

SHELLFISH

When you're approaching live 'raw' clams or mussels (as opposed to the ready-cooked vacuum-packed ones) there are a few useful things to bear in mind:

- The best way to store clams or mussels is to line a lipped baking tray with damp kitchen paper and sit the shellfish on top, making sure not to pile them up. Cover with another layer of damp kitchen paper and pop into the refrigerator.

- Before cooking shellfish, they need a little preparation. Mussels need a good scrub to clean off any dirty bits, and you need to yank off any 'beard' that is hanging around where the shells meet. To prepare clams, you need to fill a bowl with water, stir in a decent amount of salt (you're trying to replicate sea water, so be generous) and tip the clams in for about 20 minutes; they should expel any grit that may be inside. You can follow this step by putting the clams into a fresh bowl of water for 10 minutes to flush out any excess salt they may have absorbed, but this isn't essential.

- If, when you come to cook the shellfish, they don't close despite a little agitation, you need to chuck them: they're dead. Once cooked, any that did not open during the cooking process should also head to the food waste, as they're not safe to eat.

SEASONALITY

Lots of people don't realise that many fish have seasons. There are
certain times of year they must be left alone to breed and spawn, and
fish caught at this time risk damaging the fish stock in the long term.
You also risk catching fish that are too small to sell or eat. In the UK,
the Marine Conservation Society have a wonderful online tool that
gives you in-depth information on which species should be eaten and
when. Their website also includes lots of details on which fish are fine
to eat and others that are really worth steering clear of due to their
stocks being very low. If you're in North America, Seafood Watch is
a great resource for this kind of information, or try GoodFish if you're
in Australia, and Seafood New Zealand.

Different areas have different systems in place regarding fishing and fish
protection. This means that the same type of fish may be sustainable
or not sustainable, depending on where it was caught. I urge you to do
some research and make more conscientious choices with your money.
If you can, try to get down to your local fishmonger and chat to them
about what's locally caught and in season. It is also worth looking at
what is the best value for money. As most of the recipes have multiple
alternatives, make the most of what's at its best and at the best price
on the day.

READY IN
20 MINUTES

TUNA, FENNEL & BITTER LEAVES

For this dish I urge you to invest in the best tuna you can afford. Generally speaking with tinned fish, if you spend a little more you get better-tasting fish. When I eat this, it really transports me to scorching summer days in Italy spent exploring craggy coasts and stealing moments in the shade under the pine trees in the Porto Selvaggio nature reserve.

SERVES 2

160g (5¾oz) can or jar tuna in olive oil, oil reserved

1 fennel bulb, any tough outer leaves and core discarded, thinly sliced

1 tablespoon currants

2 tablespoons toasted pine nuts

3 sun-dried tomatoes, finely chopped

small handful fresh flat-leaf parsley, leaves chopped

juice of ½ lemon

1 head of chicory, roughly shredded

1 banana shallot, finely sliced

sea salt and freshly ground black pepper

Preheat your oven to 200°C/400°F/gas mark 6. In an extra-small roasting tin, toss the fennel in the reserved oil from the tuna along with 3 tablespoons of water. Season with salt and black pepper and roast for 20 minutes until soft and looking gorgeously golden and glossy.

While the fennel is roasting, soak the currants in boiling water. When the fennel is ready, drain the currants and mix into the fennel, along with the tuna, pine nuts, sun-dried tomatoes, parsley, lemon juice, chicory and shallot.

ALSO WORKS WELL WITH

Canned smoked mackerel fillets

GRILLED SQUID & COURGETTE PANZANELLA

Taking inspiration from the classic Italian panzanella salad, this very unorthodox version is home to the king of vegetables: the courgette (you may disagree, but I love them). The courgette works perfectly with the garlicky squid, and of course the classic panzanella elements of tomatoes and bread (which actually becomes toast in this recipe).

SERVES 2

2 small courgettes, sliced

3 tablespoons olive oil, plus a little extra to drizzle

zest and juice of 1 unwaxed lemon

1 garlic clove, crushed

1 tablespoon capers, roughly chopped

2 whole squid (about 350g/12oz total weight), cleaned and cut into 1.5cm (⅝in) rings, tentacles separated from the body and kept whole

75g (2¾oz) stale bread, torn into 4cm (1½in) chunks

100g (3½oz) cherry tomatoes, halved

1 shallot, finely diced

handful fresh basil, leaves roughly torn

sea salt and freshly ground black pepper

Preheat your grill to high (if you have a combined grill, place the oven shelf in a high position). In a medium-sized roasting tin, toss the courgettes with 1 tablespoon of the olive oil. Season and then pop under the grill for about 9 minutes, tossing from time to time – the courgette slices should be tender and bronzed.

Meanwhile, in a small bowl or jug, mix together the lemon zest and juice, garlic, capers and remaining olive oil. Season and set aside.

In a large bowl, drizzle a little oil over the squid and bread. Season and toss together, then arrange on top of the courgettes in the roasting tin. Grill for a further 3–4 minutes until the squid is just cooked and the bread is turning golden. Remove from the heat and mix in the tomatoes, shallot and basil, then pour over the dressing. Tuck in straight away!

ALSO WORKS WELL WITH

Raw prawns

Live mussels

Live clams

ANCHOVY, RICOTTA & SPINACH BAKED EGGS

These baked eggs are inspired by the Fiorentina pizza, which is topped with spinach and an egg. As a child, I was always full of wonder at the idea of a 'fried egg' on top of a pizza!

SERVES 2

300g (10½oz) baby spinach

250g (9oz) ricotta

zest of ½ unwaxed lemon, plus lemon wedges to serve

pinch of ground nutmeg

1 garlic clove, crushed

100g (3½oz) cherry tomatoes, halved

4 medium eggs

3 tablespoons grated Parmesan cheese

6 tinned (or jarred) anchovy fillets, roughly chopped

sea salt and freshly ground black pepper

Preheat your oven to 220°C/425°F/gas mark 7. Put the spinach into a colander and pour over a kettle of boiling water. Using a wooden spoon, squeeze out any excess water, then transfer the spinach to an extra-small roasting tin. Add the ricotta, lemon zest, nutmeg and garlic. Mix well to combine, then season. Dot the tomato halves about. Make 4 little hollows in the mixture and crack an egg into each. Top the contents of the roasting tin with the Parmesan and anchovies.

Bake in the oven for about 10 minutes, or until the egg whites have set and the cheese is turning golden. Serve with lemon wedges on the side for squeezing.

ALSO WORKS WELL WITH

Hot-smoked mackerel fillets, flesh flaked and skin discarded

Hot-smoked salmon fillets, flesh flaked and skin discarded

Hot-smoked trout fillets, flesh flaked and skin discarded

GRILLED MACKEREL
WITH BEETROOT & MUSTARD CRÈME FRAÎCHE

On a recent trip to Dublin, I had some exceptionally delicious grilled mackerel, served with a simple tomato salad, that quite honestly made me reassess how I felt about this fish. Here, gloriously oily mackerel is served up with sharp crème fraîche and sweet, mellow beetroot.

SERVES 2

juice of 1 lemon

1 large shallot, finely diced

4 precooked beetroots (about 250g/9oz in total), sliced

250g (9oz) pouch Puy lentils

4 mackerel fillets (about 100g/3½oz each)

1 tablespoon olive oil

5 tablespoons crème fraîche

2 teaspoons Dijon mustard

2 teaspoons runny honey

5 tarragon sprigs, leaves chopped

sea salt and freshly ground black pepper

Preheat your grill to high (if you have a combined grill, place the oven shelf in a medium–high position). In a small bowl, combine the lemon juice and shallot, then set aside.

Place the beetroots and lentils in a small roasting tin, then lie the mackerel on top skin-side up. Drizzle them with the oil and season. Pop the roasting tin under the grill for about 5 minutes until the mackerel skin is looking blistered and the flesh is opaque.

While the fish cooks, combine the crème fraîche and mustard in a small bowl and set aside. Mix the honey and tarragon into the shallot and lemon juice mixture.

Serve the fish, lentils and beetroots drizzled with the shallot dressing, with a dollop of the crème fraîche mix on top.

ALSO WORKS WELL WITH

Trout fillets

Butterflied sardines: 2–3 per person is perfect (they'll cook quicker, so check them after 3 minutes)

GARLIC & BAY SEAFOOD

Sweet bay and garlic are magical partners to seafood. This dish brings back memories of garlicky prawns devoured in Spain with sticky fingers. Have a good chunk of bread standing by: the dunking potential is high.

SERVES 2

2 whole squid (about 350g/12oz total weight), cleaned

6 shell-on King prawns

75g (2¾oz) slightly salted butter, cut into little pieces

1 fresh bay leaf

4 garlic cloves, crushed

zest of 1 unwaxed lemon, plus wedges to serve

½ teaspoon chilli flakes

100g (3½oz) raw mussels, prepared according to the instructions on page 16

100ml (3½fl oz) white wine or fish stock

handful fresh flat-leaf parsley, leaves roughly chopped

5 tarragon sprigs, leaves chopped

sea salt and freshly ground black pepper

bread or toast, to serve

Preheat your oven to 200°C/400°F/gas mark 6. Give the squid a rinse and pat it dry. Make about 10 incisions into one edge of each body (a bit like a hasselback potato). Separate the tentacles and keep them whole.

In a medium-sized roasting tin, toss together the prawns, squid, butter, bay, garlic, lemon zest and chilli flakes. Season, then pop into the oven for 6 minutes, giving it a little toss after 2 minutes.

Remove the roasting tin from the oven and add the mussels and wine or fish stock, then return it to the oven for a further 3 minutes.

Remove from the oven, sprinkle over the parsley and tarragon and serve with some lemon wedges for squeezing, and bread or toast for soaking up the juices.

ALSO WORKS WELL WITH

Large raw scallops

Defrosted or fresh lobster tails

Live clams

PLAICE ON CRUSHED HARISSA PEAS & BROAD BEANS

This dish is perfect for balmy summer evenings. The sweet pea and broad bean crush is elevated by the warm hum of the harissa, the fragrant herbs and the rich sharpness of crème fraîche. If you want to make this meal a little bulkier, you can serve some sautéed or boiled potatoes alongside.

SERVES 2

150g (5½oz) frozen peas

150g (5½oz) frozen broad beans

2 plaice fillets (about 180g/6¼oz each)

25g (1oz) unsalted butter

3 tablespoons crème fraîche

2 teaspoons rose harissa paste

3 mint sprigs, leaves chopped (about 2 tablespoons chopped leaves)

small handful fresh dill, chopped

zest of 1 unwaxed lemon, plus wedges to serve

sea salt and freshly ground black pepper

Preheat your grill to medium–high (if you have a combined grill, place the oven shelf in a high position). Put the peas and broad beans into a pan or large bowl and pour in a full kettle of boiling water. Set aside for 5–10 minutes until they have fully defrosted, then drain.

Tip the drained peas and beans into a small roasting tin. Arrange the fish on top (making sure to cover the peas and broad beans), skin-side down and dot with the butter. Season and grill for 3–4 minutes, or until the flesh is opaque and flakes easily.

Lift the fish out of the roasting tin and on to two plates. Add the crème fraîche and harissa to the peas and broad beans still in the roasting tin and mix together, then give the mixture a crushing with a potato masher. Stir in the herbs and lemon zest and check the seasoning. Serve the fish with the green crush and a wedge of lemon.

ALSO WORKS WELL WITH

Sea bass fillets

Lemon sole fillets

SPICY PRAWNS & SHREDDED VEG WITH RICE NOODLES

This makes a great summer supper or lunch. The fresh, zingy flavours really accentuate the sweetness of the prawns. Have a go at making a couple of omelettes with a dash of fish sauce in the beaten egg and use this sticky mixture as the filling.

SERVES 2

1 courgette, cut into matchsticks

1 carrot, cut into matchsticks

1 tablespoon sunflower oil

125g (4½oz) instant rice noodles (thin ones or thin flat ones both work here)

150g (5½oz) raw shelled prawns

2 tablespoons sriracha sauce

2 teaspoons runny honey

4½ teaspoons light soy sauce

1 garlic clove, crushed

15g (½oz) fresh root ginger, finely grated

1½ teaspoons fish sauce

4 spring onions, thinly shredded

handful fresh coriander, leaves roughly chopped

1 teaspoon sesame oil

sea salt and freshly ground black pepper

Preheat your oven to 240°C/475°F/gas mark 9. In a large roasting tin, mix together the courgette, carrot and sunflower oil. Season and pop into the oven for 10 minutes. Meanwhile, steep the noodles in boiling water for 3 minutes (some may take slightly longer, so check the packet instructions), then drain. Refresh in cold water and drain again; they hold lots of water, so give them a good shake to get as much off as possible.

Once the vegetables are tender, remove the roasting tin from the oven and add the prawns, sriracha, honey, soy sauce, garlic and ginger. Mix well and pop back into the oven for 3 minutes until the prawns are pink.

Remove the roasting tin from the oven and add the noodles, along with the fish sauce, spring onion and coriander. Toss well so that the noodles are coated with the juices from the tin. Drizzle with the sesame oil and serve.

ALSO WORKS WELL WITH

Live mussels

3cm (1¼in) chunks of firm white fish fillets, such as pollock, cod or hake

3cm (1¼in) chunks of salmon

OATMEAL-CRUSTED MACKEREL
WITH LEEKS & A HERB DRESSING

My dad's parents are Scottish, and he talks fondly of the roast chicken with oatmeal stuffing that his mum made when he was little. These oatmeal-crusted mackerel fillets are a nod to that mighty dish. The Scots are right to never underestimate oats.

SERVES 2

4 leeks, trimmed, halved lengthways and cut into half moons

3 tablespoons olive oil, plus extra to drizzle

60g (2¼oz) medium oatmeal

60g (2¼oz) rolled oats

1 medium egg

25g (1oz) plain flour

4 mackerel fillets (about 90g/3¼oz each), patted dry

1 tablespoon capers

handful fresh flat-leaf parsley, leaves finely chopped

4 mint sprigs, leaves finely chopped

small handful fresh dill, finely chopped

zest and juice of 1 unwaxed lemon

sea salt and freshly ground black pepper

Preheat your oven to 240°C/475°F/gas mark 9. Toss the leeks with 2 tablespoons of the olive oil in a large roasting tin, then season. Pop in the oven for 7 minutes, stirring from time to time.

Meanwhile, in a shallow bowl, mix together the oatmeal and rolled oats. In another bowl, beat the egg. Place the flour in a third bowl and season with salt and pepper. Dip the mackerel fillets into the flour, then dunk them in the egg, before finally coating them in the oat mixture.

Remove the roasting tin from the oven and push the leeks to the edges of the tin. Place the mackerel fillets into the space you've made. Drizzle them with oil and pop in the oven for 6 minutes. Flip and cook for another 4–6 minutes until the fillets are turning golden around the edges and the flesh is opaque.

While the fish cooks, mix together the capers, herbs, lemon juice and zest and remaining 1 tablespoon olive oil in a small bowl or jug. Season with salt and pepper.

Remove the roasting tin from the oven and serve the leeks and fish drizzled with the dressing.

ALSO WORKS WELL WITH

Butterflied sardines: 2–3 per person (these will need slightly less cooking time, about 9 minutes in total)

HOT-SMOKED SALMON SALAD
WITH APPLE, POTATO & CUCUMBER

My parents and aunty share an allotment, and it's one of my favourite places. In the summer, they grow cucumbers and we always end up with hundreds. This dish is something that evolved out of the necessity for copious cucumber consumption, but it is so delicious that I thought it deserved to be shared.

SERVES 4

450g (1lb) Charlotte potatoes (or similar waxy salad potatoes), cut into 2cm (¾in) chunks

2 tablespoons olive oil

3 fillets hot-smoked salmon (about 100g/3½oz each)

1 small cucumber, deseeded and cut into thick half-moon slices

1 green apple, quartered, cored and finely sliced

1 little gem or similar type of lettuce (about 150g/5½oz), leaves separated

sea salt and freshly ground black pepper

FOR THE DRESSING

1½ teaspoons Dijon mustard

3 teaspoons cider vinegar or white wine vinegar

6 tarragon sprigs, leaves finely chopped

zest of 1 unwaxed lemon

½ teaspoon honey

Preheat your oven to 220°C/425°F/gas mark 7. In a small roasting tin, toss the potatoes with the oil and 2 tablespoons of water. Season, then roast for 15 minutes.

Meanwhile, mix together the dressing ingredients in a small bowl or jug and set aside.

Once the potatoes have been roasting for 15 minutes, remove the roasting tin from the oven and add the salmon. Reduce the oven temperature to 180°C/350°F/gas mark 4, and return to the oven for a final 5 minutes.

To assemble the salad, flake the salmon into the potatoes, discarding the skin. Mix in the cucumber, apple and lettuce leaves, and toss with the dressing before serving.

ALSO WORKS WELL WITH

Hot-smoked trout fillets

Hot-smoked mackerel fillets

Salmon fillets (these would require an additional 5–10 minutes to cook)

SPICE-RUBBED SQUID ON GRILLED TOMATOES

This dish makes for a perfect lunch or starter. You could make it into a fuller meal by serving it up with some bread or rice alongside. Squid is the ultimate fast food! You want to keep an eagle eye on it, as it will overcook very quickly and turn into an unpleasant rubber-band-like critter.

SERVES 2

400g (14oz) medium-sized tomatoes, halved (or sliced if a little larger)

2½ tablespoons coconut oil

1 red chilli, sliced

1 teaspoon cumin seeds

2 whole squid (about 350g/12oz total weight), cleaned and cut into 1.5cm (⅝in) rings, tentacles separated from the body and kept whole

¼ teaspoon ground ginger

½ teaspoon ground coriander

small handful fresh coriander, leaves roughly torn

½ lime, cut into wedges

sea salt and freshly ground black pepper

Preheat your oven to 240°C/475°F/gas mark 9. In a medium-sized roasting tin, toss the tomatoes with the coconut oil, the chilli and the cumin seeds, then season. Pop in the oven for 8–10 minutes, giving it a shake every now and then, until the tomatoes are beginning to collapse and catch at the edges.

Meanwhile, in a large bowl, toss the squid in the ground ginger and coriander. Season with salt and black pepper.

Remove the roasting tin from the oven and add the squid. Roast for a further 2–3 minutes until the squid is just cooked (it should turn opaque). If in doubt, undercook it, because the squid will continue to cook in the residual heat of the roasting tin. Sprinkle over the fresh coriander and squeeze over the lime. Tuck in straight away!

ALSO WORKS WELL WITH

Raw prawns

Live mussels

Live clams

SALMON WITH A SIMPLE SOY & GINGER DRESSING

This light and bright salmon dish is so satisfying but doesn't leave you feeling weighed down. Try mixing up the vegetables you use – pretty much any green veg will do!

SERVES 2

½ large sweetheart cabbage (about 450g/1lb), tough core removed and cut into slim wedges

2 tablespoons sunflower oil

2 salmon fillets (about 120g/4¼oz each)

400g (14oz) can cannellini beans, drained and rinsed

sesame seeds, to sprinkle

sea salt and freshly ground black pepper

FOR THE DRESSING

4 teaspoons mirin

2 teaspoons (about 20g/¾oz) fresh root ginger, grated

2 small garlic cloves, crushed

4 teaspoons rice or cider vinegar

8 teaspoons light soy sauce

4 teaspoons sesame oil

Preheat your oven to 240°C/475°F/gas mark 9. Put the cabbage wedges into a large roasting tin and toss with the sunflower oil and 3 tablespoons of water. Season and pop the roasting tin into the oven for about 10 minutes, turning the cabbage wedges now and then until tender and beginning to look burnished. Meanwhile, mix together the dressing ingredients in a small bowl or jug.

Remove the roasting tin from the oven and place the salmon on top of the cabbage, skin-side up. Season and cook for 5 minutes.

Remove the tin from the oven once again and stir in the cannellini beans. Spoon about a third of the dressing over the salmon. Return to the oven for about 4 minutes until the fish flakes easily.

Remove from the oven and drizzle with the remaining dressing, then sprinkle over some sesame seeds and serve.

ALSO WORKS WELL WITH
Mackerel fillets

Firm white fish fillets such as pollack, pollock, haddock, tilapia or hake

PARCELS OF TILAPIA, CARROTS, ORANGE, BLACK BEANS & BAY

Let's take a moment to celebrate bay leaves, which are possibly my favourite herb. They bring such a wonderful, floral, sweet and almost piney tone to savoury dishes and puddings alike. If you have any outside space, get yourself a little bay tree in a pot: it is a very easy-going plant, happy outdoors all year round, and doesn't need any special treatment. That way, you can just pick a leaf whenever you need one. The bay in this recipe works beautifully with the orange and smoky chipotle to bring a subtle fragrance to the tilapia, carrot and beans.

SERVES 2

400g (14oz) can black beans, drained and rinsed

1 large carrot, cut into very thin half moons

2 fresh bay leaves

2 wide strips of zest and some juice from 1 unwaxed orange

2 tilapia fillets (about 130g/4¾oz) each)

generous pinch of ground coriander

2 teaspoons good-quality chipotle paste

4 teaspoons olive oil

sea salt and freshly ground black pepper

lime wedges, to serve

corn tortillas, soured cream and shredded red or white cabbage, to serve (optional)

Preheat your oven to 200°C/400°F/gas mark 6. Take 2 large pieces of foil (each about 30x45cm/12x17¾in) and lay them out on the work surface. Divide the beans between them, placing them in a mound towards one side of each piece of foil. Arrange the carrot slices on top, then top each pile with a bay leaf, a strip of orange zest and a tilapia fillet. Rub the fish fillets with the ground coriander and chipotle paste, then season. Drizzle with the olive oil and squeeze over a little orange juice.

Fold the foil over and scrunch the sides to form 2 parcels. Pop the parcels into a large roasting tin and bake for 15–17 minutes. When you open up your steaming parcels, the fish should be opaque and flake easily. Serve with the lime wedges – and some corn tortillas, soured cream and shredded white or red cabbage, if you fancy.

ALSO WORKS WELL WITH

Firm white fish fillets such as sea bass, pollack, pollock, haddock, monkfish or hake

CORNFLAKED FISH GOUJONS
WITH STICKY TOMATOES

Fish fingers are a regular go-to for me, whether in a sandwich, with rice and katsu sauce, or taking pride of place in a classic English–Italian Milanese. The fish fingers here can be used in all of those scenarios. The sweet crunch of cornflakes complements the delicate fish perfectly, while the tangy tomatoes offer contrast and punch.

SERVES 2

400g (14oz) cherry tomatoes

2 teaspoons olive oil

2 teaspoons red wine vinegar

pinch of chilli flakes

40g (1½oz) cornflakes, crushed

1 medium egg, beaten

3 tablespoons plain flour

spray oil

2 haddock fillets (about 120g/4¼oz each), cut lengthways into 2.5cm (1in) strips

sea salt and freshly ground black pepper

1 lemon, cut into wedges, to serve

FOR THE MAYONNAISE

4 tablespoons mayonnaise

handful fresh basil, leaves finely chopped

½ tablespoon capers, roughly chopped

Preheat your oven to 240°C/475°F/gas mark 9. In a medium-sized roasting tin, toss the tomatoes with the olive oil, vinegar and chilli flakes. Season, then roast for 10 minutes until looking juicy and a little charred in places.

Meanwhile, place the cornflakes in one bowl, the egg in another and the flour in a third; season with salt and black pepper. Dip a strip of haddock into the flour, then the egg, and finally dredge in the cornflakes. Set aside on a plate and repeat with the rest of the haddock.

Remove the roasting tin from the oven and push the tomatoes to one side of the tin. Line the space you've created with a piece of foil and fold it up little at the edge where it meets the tomatoes so that it acts as a divider. Transfer the fish goujons to the foil-lined space and spray them with oil. Return the roasting tin to the oven and bake for 4 minutes, then turn the fish goujons and bake for another 3–4 minutes until the fish is opaque and flakes easily.

While the fish goujons are cooking, mix the mayonnaise with the basil and capers, then season with black pepper. When everything is ready, serve the fish goujons and sticky tomatoes with the basil and caper mayo on the side and lemon wedges, for squeezing.

ALSO WORKS WELL WITH

Firm white fish fillets, such as pollack, pollock, cod, haddock or hake

ROASTED SOY MUSHROOMS
WITH PEPPERED MACKEREL & BLACK LENTILS

My Jamie loves mushrooms. Here, they are the true
heroes, going hand in hand with softly smoky mackerel
on an earthy bed of lentils. Lentils have to be up there at
the top of my all-time favourite foods.

SERVES 3-4

700g (1lb 9oz) mixed fresh mushrooms
(chestnut, portobello, oyster, shiitake) cut into
large pieces, or left whole if small

10 lemon thyme sprigs, leaves picked (about
1½ tablespoons leaves)

2 garlic cloves, crushed

2 tablespoons olive oil

**2 x 110g (3¾oz) cans peppered smoked
mackerel, drained and oil reserved, flesh
flaked into large pieces**

1 tablespoon white miso paste

1 tablespoon light soy sauce

400g (14oz) can beluga lentils (brown or
green will also work), drained

1 teaspoon sesame oil

4 spring onions, finely sliced

1 red chilli, finely sliced

sea salt and freshly ground black pepper

TIP If you cannot find lemon thyme,
just use regular thyme, plus the zest
of ¼ unwaxed lemon.

Preheat your oven to 240°C/475°F/gas mark
9. In a large roasting tin, mix together the
mushrooms, lemon thyme, garlic, olive oil
and mackerel oil; then season. Place in the
oven and roast for 10 minutes.

Remove the tin from the oven and stir in
the miso, soy, lentils and mackerel. Return
to the oven for 5 minutes.

To serve, drizzle over the sesame oil and
sprinkle over the spring onions and chilli.

ALSO WORKS WELL WITH

Hot-smoked trout fillets, skin discarded
and flesh flaked

Hot-smoked salmon fillets, skin discarded
and flesh flaked

Salmon fillets (these would require an
additional 5–10 minutes to cook)

For all of the above, you may need to use
a little extra oil to make up for the lack of
tinned fish oil.

CURRIED SARDINES ON TOAST
WITH SHREDDED ONION

As someone who works from home a lot of the time (even before lockdowns), I'm always on the lookout for a quick, pack-a-punch lunch. This is just that: full of flavour, filling and very speedy to make.

SERVES 2

½ large onion, thinly sliced

juice of 1 lemon

2 x 120g (4¼oz) cans sardines in olive oil, drained

2 teaspoons mild curry powder

2 large slices of sourdough bread

salted butter, for spreading

1 red chilli, thinly sliced

sea salt and freshly ground black pepper

mango chutney or lime pickle, to serve

TIP Try arranging slices of tomato on top of the sardine mixture before grilling.

Preheat your grill to medium–high (if you have a combined grill, place the oven shelf in a high position). In a small bowl, steep the onion in the lemon juice and set aside. In another bowl, crush the sardines with the curry powder and season with a little salt and lots of black pepper.

Pop the bread into a small roasting tin and grill on one side, then turn and very lightly grill the other side.

Spread the lightly grilled sides of the toast with butter and top each with half of the sardine mixture, taking care to spread it right to the edges. Grill for 3–4 minutes until starting to look golden on top.

Pile the marinated onion slices and chilli on top of the sardine toasts and serve with a spoonful of mango chutney or lime pickle alongside.

ALSO WORKS WELL WITH

Tinned mackerel

Tinned smoked mackerel

GRILLED COD ON PUY LENTILS
WITH CHORIZO & LEAVES

This is a great summer salad, perfect paired with a cold, crisp lager, and eaten outside. It's a good one to double up when cooking for friends. Serve with some boiled new potatoes and whip up an aioli for a real feast (see page 124 for my homemade aioli recipe).

SERVES 2

1 lemon, halved

4 fresh oregano sprigs

2 garlic cloves, thinly sliced

about 8 thick slices of dry-cured chorizo

300g (10½oz) medium-sized tomatoes, sliced

2 tablespoons olive oil

1 teaspoon smoked paprika, plus extra for sprinkling

2 cod fillets (about 150g/5½oz each)

250g (9oz) pouch cooked Puy lentils (or canned green or brown lentils)

handful of mixed salad leaves

sea salt and freshly ground black pepper

Preheat your oven to 240°C/475°F/gas mark 9. Toss the lemon halves, oregano, garlic, chorizo and tomatoes in a medium-sized roasting tin with the olive oil and paprika. Season and pop into the oven for 6–8 minutes, giving the tin a shake now and then, until the tomatoes look burnished.

Remove the roasting tin from the oven and arrange the fish on top of the tomatoes. Season again, then pop back into the oven for a further 6–8 minutes until the fish is opaque and flakes easily.

Lift the fish out of the roasting tin and set aside on a plate. Remove the lemon halves. Gently stir the lentils into the roasting tin, then return the fish and tumble in the leaves. Squeeze over some of the roasted lemon and sprinkle with a little extra paprika, then serve.

ALSO WORKS WELL WITH

Firm white fish fillets, such as pollack, pollock, haddock, tilapia or hake

Salmon fillets

Trout fillets

TIP If you want to make this pescatarian, leave out the chorizo and add a little extra oil and paprika, as well as a few chopped canned anchovies to bring salty savouriness.

HERRING, SAUERKRAUT & WATERCRESS SALAD

This dish draws on the German Christmases of my childhood. I have flashes of memories of pickled fish and hard-boiled eggs, but there is rather more emphasis on the yearly opening of weighty chocolate letters my grandad got in Holland, greedily scoffed on the spot. A note: herring do have a habit of looking a little scary, rather like greyish lumps in liquid, but they are really tasty and worth giving a go.

SERVES 2

350g (12oz) small potatoes, cut into 2cm (¾in) chunks

2 banana shallots, each cut into 6–8 wedges

2 tablespoons olive oil

pinch of caraway seeds

165g (5¾oz) dill-marinated herring, cut into 2.5cm (1in) pieces, plus 2 tablespoons of the marinade

60g (2¼oz) sauerkraut

80g (2¾oz) watercress

1 small red apple, cut into little chunks, a similar size to the potato

sea salt and freshly ground black pepper

Preheat your oven to 220°C/425°F/gas mark 7. In a medium-sized roasting tin, toss the potatoes and shallots with the oil, caraway seeds and 2 tablespoons of water, then season and roast for 17–20 minutes.

Remove the roasting tin from the oven and stir in the herring, marinade, sauerkraut, watercress and apple. Serve.

ALSO WORKS WELL WITH

Smoked mackerel fillets

Hot-smoked trout fillets, flesh flaked and skin discarded

Hot-smoked salmon fillets, flesh flaked and skin discarded

If you're using one of these alternative fish, use the marinade from a jar of dill pickles in place of the herring marinade.

GINGER & LEMON GRASS SALMON
WITH GREENS IN A PARCEL

Cooking your fish in a parcel is a great way to keep it juicy and tender. It's a fabulous method to apply to different fish and flavours. Try using curry leaves, tomatoes and garlic or soy, chilli and a little Shaoxing wine as alternatives.

SERVES 1

1 tablespoon light soy sauce

1 tablespoon mirin

2 spring onions, thinly shredded

1 courgette, halved widthways and then cut into thin sticks

handful of sugar snap peas, halved lengthways

1 salmon fillet (about 120g/4¼oz)

1 lemon grass stalk, very thinly shredded, any tough outer leaves discarded

1 red chilli, thinly sliced

7g (¼oz) piece of fresh root ginger, finely shredded

1 garlic clove, thinly sliced

sea salt and freshly ground black pepper

handful fresh coriander, chopped, to serve

TIPS Try with a drizzle of sesame oil before serving.
This recipe is very easy to multiply: just increase the ingredients accordingly and make up as many individual parcels as needed.

Preheat your oven to 200°C/400°F/gas mark 6. In a small bowl, combine the soy and mirin. Cut a piece of greaseproof paper or foil roughly 50x40cm (20x15in) and place in a medium-sized roasting tin.

Place the spring onions, courgette and sugar snap peas on the paper and season. Place the fish on top, then top with the lemon grass, chilli, ginger and garlic. Pour over the soy-and-mirin mixture. Fold the sides of the paper over the top, joining them in the middle, and fold together, pleating to enclose. Fold the ends of the paper over several times, then tuck them underneath the parcel to secure.

Pop into the oven for 20 minutes until the fish is just opaque and flakes easily. Pop the parcel onto a plate and scatter over some coriander, before tucking in.

ALSO WORKS WELL WITH

Firm white fish fillets, such as pollack, pollock, haddock, tilapia or hake

Trout fillet

CHILLI PRAWNS & SHREDDED BRUSSELS SPROUTS
WITH GARLIC & PRESERVED LEMON MAYO

I see this dish as a perfect starter: something moreish to pick at in the sunshine. Brussels sprouts are a little divisive, but I have found that preparing them in this manner can convert even the most entrenched sprout-hater; the sprouts caramelise as they catch and are totally delicious. To make this more of a main course, serve up with some little roasted potatoes to dunk in any excess mayo – but be warned, it's addictive.

SERVES 2

200g (7oz) Brussels sprouts, thinly shredded

½ teaspoon pul biber (Aleppo chilli flakes)

20g (¾oz) unsalted butter

150g (5½oz) raw shelled prawns

small handful fresh flat-leaf parsley, finely chopped

sea salt

FOR THE GARLIC AND PRESERVED LEMON MAYO

1 garlic clove, crushed

70g (2½oz) mayonnaise

1 preserved lemon (about 25g/1oz), pith and innards discarded, finely chopped

zest of 1 unwaxed lemon, plus wedges to serve

Preheat your oven to 240°C/475°F/gas mark 9. In a medium-sized roasting tin, toss the sprouts with the pul biber flakes and dot over the butter, then season with salt and pop in the oven. Roast for 5 minutes, then toss and return to the oven for a further 3–4 minutes.

Meanwhile, mix together the garlic, mayonnaise, preserved lemon and lemon zest in a small bowl and set aside.

The sprouts should now be tender and looking burnished. Remove the roasting tin from the oven and stir in the prawns. Return to the oven for another 2 minutes.

Remove from the oven and sprinkle the parsley over the top. Serve the sprouts and prawns with the garlic mayonnaise alongside, and lemon wedges for squeezing.

ALSO WORKS WELL WITH

Raw scallops

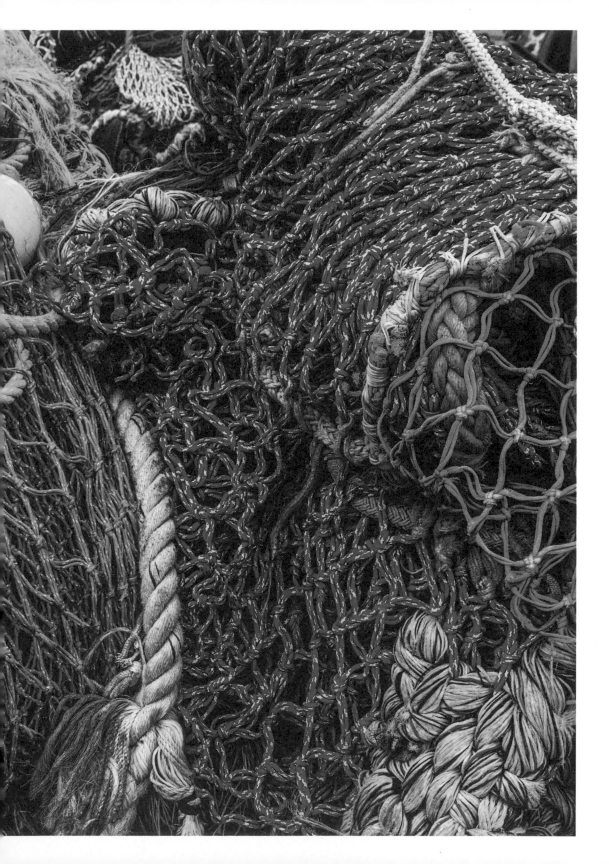

GREENS & QUINOA
WITH FLAKED KIPPERS

This light and bright salad is so quick to rustle up, it's the perfect post-work dinner. Try using different spice combinations: coriander, smoked paprika, fennel seeds and ras el hanout would all work well. Be warned: kippers are not for the bone-fearer. If you can get past this, though, their flavour is outstanding.

SERVES 2

2 kippers (about 250g/9oz each)

pinch of chilli flakes

25g (1oz) unsalted butter

250g (9oz) pouch cooked quinoa

zest and juice of 1 unwaxed lemon

1 avocado, peeled, stoned and thinly sliced

½ cucumber, sliced into half moons

100g (3½oz) sugar snap peas, halved diagonally

sea salt and freshly ground black pepper

¾ teaspoons za'atar, to serve

plain yogurt, to serve

Preheat your grill to high (if you have a combined grill, place the oven shelf in a medium–high position). Place the kippers into a small roasting tin and top with the chilli flakes and little blobs of butter. Pop the roasting tin under the grill for 3–4 minutes until the fish is hot.

Lift the kippers on to a plate and carefully remove the skin, spines and heads, then flake the fish back into the roasting tin. Tip in the quinoa and season, then pop back under the grill for 2–3 minutes.

Add the lemon zest and juice, along with the avocado, cucumber and sugar snap peas. Toss to combine before sprinkling with za'atar and serving with a dollop of yogurt.

ALSO WORKS WELL WITH

Hot-smoked mackerel fillets

Hot-smoked salmon fillets

Hot-smoked trout fillets

TROUT & SPRING ONIONS
WITH CHOPPED RED PEPPER DRESSING

This delicious sauce is inspired by Romesco, which originated in Catalonia. Traditionally made up of roasted tomatoes and peppers, garlic, nuts and oil, it is the perfect partner to the earthiness of trout. This recipe makes a generous amount of dressing, leaving you with leftovers that can be piled on to fried eggs or spooned over roast chicken – or pretty much anything else that takes your fancy.

SERVES 2

1 teaspoon fennel seeds

2 bunches of spring onions, trimmed

½ lemon, sliced

2 trout fillets (about 120g/4¼oz each)

4 tablespoons olive oil

50g (1¾oz) blanched almonds, finely chopped

100g (3½oz) roasted peppers from a jar, finely chopped

1 garlic clove, crushed

1 tablespoon sherry vinegar

1 teaspoon hot paprika

1 teaspoon tomato purée

sea salt and freshly ground black pepper

TIPS For more depth of flavour, toast the almonds in a frying pan and allow to cool before chopping.
If you like a little more heat, try adding a finely chopped red chilli to the pepper dressing.

Preheat your grill to high (if you have a combined grill, place the oven shelf in a medium–high position). Lightly bash the fennel seeds in a pestle and mortar (or roughly chop) to help to release their aroma. Place the spring onions and lemon slices into a medium-sized roasting tin. Sprinkle over the fennel seeds and place the fish on top, skin-side up. Season the contents of the roasting tin with salt and black pepper, and drizzle with 2 tablespoons of the oil.

Grill for about 4–5 minutes until the skin on the trout looks golden. Flip the fish, give the spring onions a good shake about, and cook for another 4–5 minutes until the flesh looks opaque and the spring onions are tender and charring in places. If the fish seems done sooner, just lift it out and set aside on a plate, then return the roasting tin to the grill for a couple of extra minutes.

While the fish is cooking, make the dressing. In a small bowl or jug, mix together the almonds, roasted peppers, garlic, sherry vinegar, paprika and tomato purée with the remaining olive oil (adding a little extra oil if needed). Season. Serve the grilled fish and spring onions with the sauce alongside.

ALSO WORKS WELL WITH

Mackerel fillets

Butterflied sardines: 2–3 per person is perfect (they'll cook quicker, so check them after 3 minutes)

ROASTED SALMON CAESAR

This simple salad is my version of the well-loved classic. It feels wonderfully light yet indulgent with the cheesy croutons and soured cream dressing. Feel free to garnish with extra capers or anchovy fillets for a bonus salty punch.

SERVES 4

4 slices of white sourdough (about 200g/7oz), torn into small chunks

2 tablespoons olive oil

1 tablespoon capers

4 salmon fillets (about 120g/4¼oz each)

2 tablespoons finely grated Parmesan cheese

1 large head romaine lettuce (or little gem/cos), shredded

½ cucumber, sliced into half moons

zest of ½ unwaxed lemon, plus wedges to serve

sea salt and freshly ground black pepper

FOR THE DRESSING

1 tablespoon olive oil

1 teaspoon Dijon mustard

6 canned anchovy fillets, drained and very finely chopped

1 tablespoon cider vinegar

1 small garlic clove, crushed

4 tablespoons soured cream

TIP Try stirring some soft herbs into the dressing; basil, tarragon, dill or parsley would all be delicious.

Preheat your oven to 220°C/425°F/gas mark 7. In a large roasting tin, toss the bread with the olive oil, then mix in the capers. Tuck the salmon fillets in among the bread pieces and season.

Roast for 8 minutes, then remove from the oven. Sprinkle the sourdough croutons with the Parmesan and return the tin to the oven for 3 minutes until the salmon flesh is opaque and the croutons are golden.

Meanwhile, to make the dressing, beat together the olive oil, mustard, anchovies, vinegar and garlic in a small jug or bowl. Mix in the soured cream, then season and set aside.

Remove the roasting tin from the oven and flake the fish, discarding the skin. Add the lettuce and cucumber to the tin, drizzle over the dressing and toss to combine. Grate over the lemon zest and serve with lemon wedges for squeezing.

ALSO WORKS WELL WITH

Trout fillets

Mackerel fillets

Hot-smoked salmon (this only needs 5 minutes in the oven)

Hot-smoked trout (this only needs 5 minutes in the oven)

GRILLED MACKEREL
WITH ORANGES, OLIVES & GREEN LENTILS

The sweet, salty, citrus flavours in this recipe cut perfectly through the rich, oily mackerel. This is such an elegant dish, ideal for making for a friend – or for when you want to make something that feels a bit special for yourself. Any leftovers will be delicious at room temperature, but perhaps discard the skin before tucking in.

SERVES 2

1 shallot, finely chopped

1 tablespoon sherry vinegar

2 oranges, peeled and sliced

12 green olives, sliced

4 mackerel fillets (about 90g/3¼oz each)

2 tablespoons olive oil

400g (14oz) can green lentils, drained

small handful fresh basil, leaves roughly chopped

sea salt and freshly ground black pepper

Place the shallot and vinegar in a mug or small bowl and set aside to soak.

Preheat your grill to high (if you have a combined grill, place the oven shelf in a high position). In a medium-sized roasting tin, toss together the orange slices, olives and mackerel with the olive oil and season. Once everything is coated, arrange the orange slices in a layer on the bottom of the tin, then place the mackerel on top, skin-side up.

Place the roasting tin under the grill for 4–5 minutes until the skin on the mackerel is looking blistered and the flesh is opaque.

Lift the fish out of the roasting tin and set aside on a plate. Stir the lentils into the mixture in the tin and return to the grill for 5–6 minutes until the orange slices start to catch. Place the fish back on top and pop back under the grill for about 30 seconds, just to warm the fish up a little.

Drizzle over the shallot and vinegar mixture, sprinkle over the basil and serve.

ALSO WORKS WELL WITH

Butterflied sardines: 2–3 per person is perfect (they'll cook quicker, so check them after 3 minutes)

Trout fillets

HOT-SMOKED TROUT & ROASTED ASPARAGUS SALAD
WITH HERBED OIL

This dish works well warm or cold, so it is perfect for packing up and taking to work for lunch the next day; just leave it out of the refrigerator for an hour or so before you eat it so that it can come to room temperature.

SERVES 2

400g (14oz) asparagus, woody ends removed

½ teaspoon pul biber (Aleppo chilli flakes)

6 tablespoons olive oil

handful fresh basil, leaves stripped

3 sprigs tarragon, leaves stripped

zest and juice of ½ unwaxed lemon, plus wedges to serve

1 small garlic clove, crushed

400g (14oz) can flageolet beans, drained and rinsed

2 hot-smoked trout fillets (about 125g/4½oz)

sea salt and freshly ground black pepper

bread, to serve

TIP If you want to use less oil, you can swap out 2 tablespoons for water.

Preheat your oven to 220°C/425°F/gas mark 7. In a small roasting tin, toss the asparagus with the pul biber flakes and 1 tablespoon of the olive oil. Season and roast for 8–10 minutes, shaking from time to time, until tender and turning golden.

Meanwhile, using a stick blender, blitz the herbs with the remaining olive oil, the lemon zest and the garlic. Season and add a squeeze of lemon juice.

Remove the roasting tin from the oven and stir in the beans, then flake in the fish. Pop back into the oven for 2 minutes to warm through, then drizzle over the dressing and serve with a wedge of lemon and a hunk of bread on the side.

ALSO WORKS WELL WITH

Hot-smoked salmon fillets

Trout fillets (these will need to go into the oven at the same time as the asparagus)

Salmon fillets (these will need to go into the oven at the same time as the asparagus)

VIETNAMESE-STYLE TURMERIC SALMON
WITH DILL & RICE NOODLES

I first tried a version of this dish while testing recipes for a food magazine. This flavour combination is so, so delicious. I feel that the fatty salmon brings a certain indulgence; traditionally, white fish is used.

SERVES 2

½ tablespoon ground turmeric

30g (1oz) piece fresh root ginger, finely grated

3 tablespoons sunflower oil

1 onion, thinly sliced

2 garlic cloves, crushed

2 salmon fillets (about 120g/4¼oz each), skin removed, cut into roughly 2.5cm (1in) chunks

100g (3½oz) thin rice noodles, soaked in boiling water according to packet instructions

handful fresh dill, finely chopped

30g (1oz) roasted and salted peanuts, roughly chopped

sea salt and freshly ground black pepper

FOR THE DRESSING

4 teaspoons fish sauce

juice of 1 lime

4 teaspoons soft brown sugar

1 red chilli, deseeded and finely chopped

1 garlic clove, crushed

Preheat your oven to 220°C/425°F/gas mark 7. In a small roasting tin, mix together the turmeric, ginger, oil, onion and garlic. Roast for 12 minutes.

Remove the roasting tin from the oven and mix in the salmon and 2 tablespoons of water; season lightly. Return to the oven and cook for a further 6–8 minutes, until the salmon is just cooked through.

Meanwhile, make the dressing. Place all the dressing ingredients plus 2 tablespoons of water in a small jug or bowl and mix well to combine.

When the salmon is ready, add the noodles and dill to the roasting tin and toss to coat in all of the juices, then drizzle over the dressing. Sprinkle with the peanuts and serve.

ALSO WORKS WELL WITH

Firm white fish fillets, such as pollack, pollock, haddock, tilapia or hake

READY IN
30 MINUTES

SEVEN-SPICE SARDINES & CAULIFLOWER
WITH GARLIC YOGURT

On the banks of the Golden Horn in Istanbul, little stalls fill the air with the glorious smell of grilling fish. The fish is served up in bread rolls with lettuce, slim slices of onion and a good squeeze of lemon juice. Scores of fishermen line the Galata Bridge in the buzzing centre of Istanbul, fishing, chatting and sharing drinks. It's such a magical thing to find in the middle of a giant city.

SERVES 2

½ red onion, thinly sliced

juice of ½ lemon, plus wedges to serve

1 cauliflower (about 600g/1lb 5oz), broken into small florets, with any leaves saved and stalk chopped up

2 tablespoons olive oil

4 butterflied sardines, about 200g (7oz) total weight

1 teaspoon Baharat (seven-spice mix)

½ teaspoon dried mint

handful fresh flat-leaf parsley, leaves chopped

sea salt and freshly ground black pepper

FOR THE GARLIC YOGURT

125g (4½oz) plain yogurt

1 small garlic clove, crushed

zest of 1 unwaxed lemon

Preheat your oven to 190°C/375°F/gas mark 5. In a small bowl, submerge the onion in the lemon juice and set aside.

Toss the cauliflower florets and any leaves and stalk with the olive oil and 1 tablespoon of water in a large roasting tin. Season and roast for about 20 minutes until tender and burnished at the edges.

While the cauliflower is roasting, make the garlic yogurt. In a small bowl, combine the yogurt, garlic and lemon zest; season and set aside.

Remove the roasting tin from the oven and preheat your grill to high. Pop the sardines into a bowl and rub with the Baharat and dried mint, along with some salt and black pepper. Lie the sardines skin-side up on top of the cauliflower. Grill for 3 minutes until the flesh is opaque and the skin is blistered.

Sprinkle the marinated onions and parsley over the top and serve with the garlic yogurt and lemon wedges on the side, for squeezing.

ALSO WORKS WELL WITH

Whole sardines: cut a few slashes into each side before grilling

Whole mackerel (you'll only need 2): cut slashes into the skin before grilling; these will need about 5–6 minutes per side

Mackerel fillets: these should take about 5 minutes to grill

ROASTED COURGETTE
WITH TUNA & FLAGEOLET BEANS

Not much beats a roasted courgette: sweet, crisp, soft and utterly delicious. This salad is something I make throughout the summer months. Experiment with using different canned beans or try smoked mackerel in place of tuna.

SERVES 2

3 small courgettes, cut into chunky rounds

2 tablespoons olive oil

½ teaspoon fennel seeds

400g (14oz) can flageolet beans, drained and rinsed

160g (5¾oz) can tuna in olive oil, drained

1 tablespoon capers, roughly chopped

small handful fresh mint leaves, finely chopped

1 red chilli, finely chopped

zest and juice of 1 unwaxed lemon

sea salt and freshly ground black pepper

Preheat your oven to 240°C/475°F/gas mark 9. In a large roasting tin, toss the courgettes with the olive oil and fennel seeds. Season and pop in the oven for about 20 minutes, turning halfway through.

Once the courgettes are looking golden, remove the roasting tin from the oven and tip in the beans. Stir and return to the oven for 3 minutes. Finally, stir in the tuna, capers, mint, chilli and lemon zest and juice and serve.

ALSO WORKS WELL WITH

Smoked mackerel

Tinned mackerel

Crab meat

Hot-smoked salmon fillets, flesh flaked and skin discarded

Hot-smoked trout fillets, flesh flaked and skin discarded

SOY & BLACK-PEPPER PRAWNS
WITH CORN RICE

I always feel compelled to make things with sweetcorn;
I love the stuff. This year, my mum and dad grew
sweetcorn on their allotment for the first time, and it
was delicious. You could use fresh corn in this recipe but
I've suggested tinned for its reliable year-round flavour
and availability. This dish is wonderfully sweet and
fragrant, with a little spicy punch from the black pepper.

SERVES 2

2 tablespoons sunflower oil

1 large banana shallot, thinly sliced

1 fresh bay leaf

1 star anise

1 teaspoon soft brown sugar

125g (4½oz) white basmati rice

300ml (10fl oz) boiling water

198g (7oz) can sweetcorn, drained

165g (5¾oz) raw shelled prawns

light soy sauce, to taste

sea salt and freshly ground black pepper

Preheat your oven to 220°C/425°F/gas mark
7. Tip the oil into a small roasting tin. Add the
shallot, bay leaf, star anise and brown sugar
and roast for 5–10 minutes, stirring from time
to time, until golden. Remove from the oven
and tip in the rice, along with a good pinch of
salt and the boiling water. Cover with foil and
bake for 15 minutes.

Turn the oven off and remove the roasting
tin. Peel back the foil, stir the rice and mix
through the sweetcorn and prawns. Replace
the foil and pop back into the oven for 5–7
minutes until the prawns turn pink, they will
cook in the residual heat of the oven. Grind
over lots of black pepper and drip over some
soy sauce before serving.

ALSO WORKS WELL WITH

Live mussels

Live clams

SMOKED MACKEREL, FENNEL & POTATOES
WITH A KAFFIR LIME LEAF DRESSING

The smoked fish in this recipes works so well with the highly fragrant dressing, while the potatoes act as a wonderful sponge and the fennel brings a mellow aniseed crunch. Try stirring a tablespoon or two of coconut milk into the dressing if you fancy a little extra sweetness.

SERVES 2

350g (12oz) potatoes, cut into roughly 2cm (¾in) chunks

2 x 110g (3¾oz) cans smoked mackerel, oil reserved

½ tablespoon olive or sunflower oil

1 large fennel bulb, any tough outer leaves and core discarded, cut as thinly as possible

4 spring onions, thinly sliced

sea salt and freshly ground black pepper

FOR THE DRESSING

4 teaspoons fish sauce

juice and zest of 1 unwaxed lime

4 teaspoons soft brown sugar

2 red chillies, deseeded and finely chopped

1 garlic clove, crushed

2 fresh kaffir lime leaves, thinly sliced

Preheat your oven to 220°C/425°F/gas mark 7. In a small roasting tin, toss the potatoes with the reserved mackerel oil and olive oil. Season and roast for 20–25 minutes until golden and tender.

Meanwhile, make your dressing by mixing together all the dressing ingredients with 2 tablespoons of water in a small jug or bowl. Set aside.

When the potatoes are ready, flake in the fish and stir through the fennel, spring onions and dressing. Serve.

ALSO WORKS WELL WITH

Fresh smoked mackerel, flesh flaked and skin discarded

Hot-smoked salmon fillets, flesh flaked and skin discarded

Hot-smoked trout fillets, flesh flaked and skin discarded

For all of the above, increase the oil for roasting the potatoes to 2 tablespoons to make up for the lack of canned fish oil.

LEMON SOLE
WITH BRAISED LETTUCE, PEAS & PANCETTA

This dish is a summery number, a beautiful celebration of green. I have strong memories of a giant lemon sole I had in a tiny fish restaurant in Glasgow: the fish was so big it only just fitted on the table! It was served simply, covered in brown shrimp and butter with a side of crisp fries; it was divine. You could make some little roast potatoes or a roasting tin of oven chips to go alongside this fish for the full restaurant experience.

SERVES 2

50g (1¾oz) unsalted butter, cut into little chunks

70g (2½oz) chopped pancetta

4 shallots, chopped

1 garlic clove, sliced

2 little gem lettuces, cut into quarters

200g (7oz) frozen petit pois

400ml (14fl oz) vegetable stock

1 lemon sole (roughly 600g/1lb 5oz), scaled and gutted

zest of 1 unwaxed lemon, plus wedges to serve

sea salt and freshly ground black pepper

Preheat your oven to 220°C/425°F/gas mark 7. Place the butter, pancetta, shallots and garlic in a large roasting tin and pop into the oven for 15 minutes. The shallots and garlic should be soft and turning golden, and the pancetta crisp, having rendered its fat. Add the lettuce, toss it in the fat and return the roasting tin to the oven for 5 minutes.

Remove from the oven and tip in the frozen peas, stirring to combine. Lie the fish on top, skin-side up. Season the fish and bake for about 10 minutes or until the fish flesh is opaque. Sprinkle over the lemon zest and serve with lemon wedges.

ALSO WORKS WELL WITH
Another flat fish, such as Dover sole, dab, plaice or brill

TIP If you want to make this pescatarian, leave out the pancetta and add a little extra butter at the start of the recipe, along with a few chopped canned anchovies for salty savouriness.

SALMON WITH GRAPEFRUIT, HARISSA & CAPERS

This dish makes for a brilliant summer supper. It's a wonderful balance of sweet, sharp and salty, with a gentle warmth from the harissa. If you like, you can try swapping the butter beans for cannellini beans, boiled potatoes or chickpeas.

SERVES 4

2 teaspoons rose harissa

1 ripe pink grapefruit, peeled with as much pith removed as possible, segmented and cut into small chunks

2 fennel bulbs, any tough outer leaves and core discarded, cut into thin wedges, fronds reserved

3 tablespoons capers

5 tablespoons olive oil, plus extra to drizzle

400g (14oz) can butter beans, drained

4 salmon fillets (about 120g/4¼oz each)

small handful fresh flat-leaf parsley, leaves roughly chopped

small handful fresh mint, leaves roughly chopped

sea salt and freshly ground black pepper

lemon wedges, to serve

Preheat your oven to 220°C/425°F/gas mark 7. In a large roasting tin, mix together the harissa, grapefruit, fennel and capers. Spoon over the 5 tablespoons of olive oil and 2 tablespoons of water, then season, cover with foil and cook for 20 minutes.

Increase the oven temperature to 230°C/450°F/gas mark 8. Take out the roasting tin and stir in the butter beans. Add the salmon, turning to coat in the juices before positioning flesh-side up, drizzle with a little extra olive oil and season. Return the tin to the oven for about 8 minutes until the flesh flakes easily.

Sprinkle the roasting tin with the herbs and fennel fronds and serve with lemon wedges for squeezing.

ALSO WORKS WELL WITH

Trout fillets

Firm white fish fillets, such as pollack, pollock, haddock, tilapia or hake

TIPS If you're not a grapefruit fan, you could make this with a large orange instead.
To check for ripeness when buying a grapefruit, give it a good sniff. If it has a strong grapefruit-y aroma, you're good to go!

PEPPERS & AUBERGINE
WITH ANCHOVIES & OLIVES

This dish gains its depth and umami addictiveness from the anchovies melted within. It absolutely doesn't scream fish, so even fish sceptics should enjoy this one. It is delicious piled on to toast, stirred through pasta or as a side dish to roast chicken or sausages.

SERVES 4

2 red, yellow or orange peppers, cut into 2.5cm (1in) pieces

2 aubergines, cut into 2.5cm (1in) pieces

300g (10½oz) cherry tomatoes

6 tablespoons olive oil

50g (1¾oz) can anchovies, drained and finely chopped

1 tablespoon white wine vinegar

3 garlic cloves, thinly sliced

15 kalamata olives, stones removed, roughly chopped

small handful fresh dill, chopped

small handful fresh flat-leaf parsley, leaves chopped

sea salt and freshly ground black pepper

bread, to serve

Preheat your oven to 230°C/450°F/gas mark 8. In a large roasting tin, toss together the peppers, aubergines, tomatoes, olive oil, anchovies, vinegar, garlic and olives. Season with a little salt and black pepper.

Pop the roasting tin into the oven for 25 minutes, stirring now and then, until the vegetables are soft and turning golden. Remove from the oven and stir in the herbs. Check the seasoning; it may need a little extra salt or vinegar. Serve with the bread alongside.

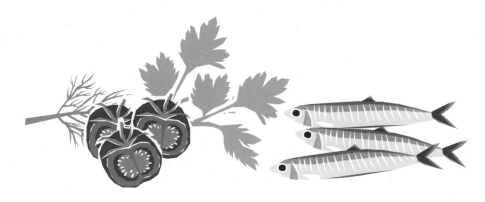

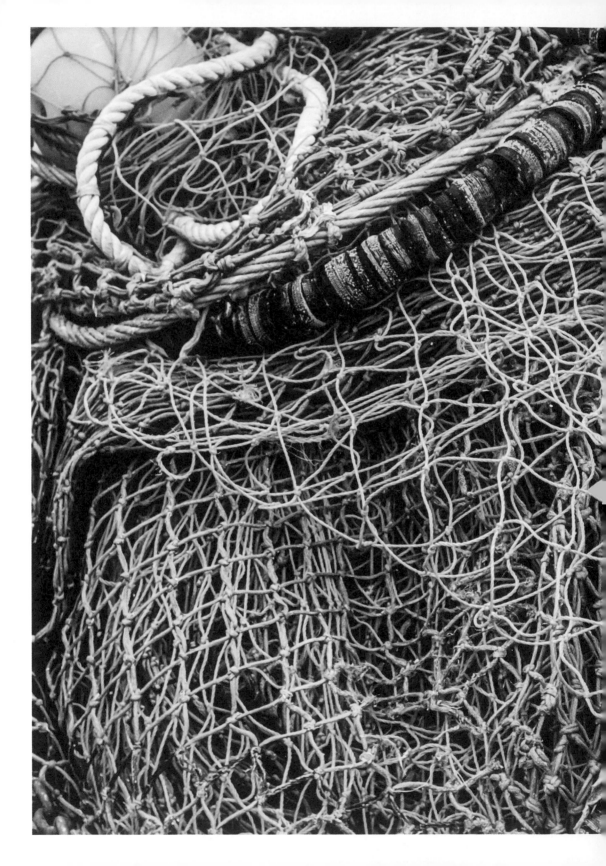

SMOKY CHILLI & TOMATO MUSSELS

The smokiness of the chilli here helps the sweetness of the mussels sing. This is a super-speedy supper that feels like so much more than the sum of its parts. Surprisingly, mussels are fairly inexpensive, so 'treat' yourself!

SERVES 2

2 tablespoons olive oil

1 onion, thinly sliced

1 celery stick, thinly sliced

1 teaspoon ancho chilli flakes

½ cinnamon stick

½ teaspoon cumin seeds

1 garlic clove, finely sliced

2 x 400g (14oz) cans whole plum tomatoes

400g (14oz) can white beans (cannellini or haricot), drained and rinsed

750g (1lb 10oz) live mussels, prepared according to the instructions on page 16

zest and juice of 1 unwaxed lime

small handful of fresh coriander, leaves torn

sea salt and freshly ground black pepper

bread or toast, to serve

Preheat your oven to 220°C/425°F/gas mark 7. In a medium-sized roasting tin, toss together the oil, onion and celery and pop in the oven for 10 minutes or so until the onion and celery have softened and are beginning to turn golden.

Remove the roasting tin from the oven and add the chilli flakes, cinnamon stick, cumin seeds and garlic. Return to the oven for a couple of minutes, then add the tomatoes and white beans. Season and pop back into the oven for 12–15 minutes.

Remove the roasting tin from the oven once more and stir in the mussels. Return to the oven for a final 3–4 minutes until the mussels have sprung open (remember to discard any that remain closed). Top with the lime zest and juice and coriander, and serve with bread or toast.

ALSO WORKS WELL WITH

Live clams

Cooked mussels or clams (add at the same point as you would the live mussels, so they have time to warm through)

HAZELNUT-CRUSTED POLLOCK
WITH BAY-ROASTED COURGETTES

This dish can easily be doubled; just increase the tin size and double all the ingredients. You want to give the courgettes plenty of space so that they get nicely browned and don't just sweat – if in doubt, use a bigger roasting tin. I love the combination of the nutty, crunchy topping with sweet, soft courgettes.

SERVES 2

2 courgettes (about 400g/14oz total weight), cut into thick discs

2 tablespoons olive oil

2 fresh bay leaves

2 slim slices of brown bread, crumbled into small pieces (or 50g/1¾oz fresh breadcrumbs)

zest of 1 unwaxed lemon, plus lemon wedges, to serve

¼ teaspoon fennel seeds, crushed

20g (¾oz) blanched hazelnuts, chopped

250g (9oz) pouch cooked Puy lentils (or you can use canned brown or green lentils)

100ml (3½fl oz) dry vermouth (I use Noilly Prat)

2 pollock fillets (about 120g/4¼oz each)

sea salt and freshly ground black pepper

Preheat your oven to 240°C/475°F/gas mark 9. In a large roasting tin, toss the courgette slices with 1 tablespoon of the oil. Tuck in the bay leaves and season, then roast for 15–20 minutes, turning halfway; the courgettes should be tender and turning golden.

Meanwhile, toss the breadcrumbs with the remaining 1 tablespoon oil, along with the lemon zest, fennel seeds and hazelnuts.

Remove the roasting tin from the oven and stir in the lentils, vermouth and 2 tablespoons of water. Place the fish on top, then scatter over the breadcrumbs. Reduce the oven temperature to 210°C/410°F/gas mark 6 and bake for 10–12 minutes until the fish is opaque and flakes easily. Serve with the lemon wedges.

ALSO WORKS WELL WITH
Firm white fish fillets, such as cod, hake, haddock or tilapia

CRAB & TARRAGON TART

This super-simple tart is a great make-ahead lunch or summer supper. Pack it up and take it picnicking, cold, or tuck in while it's warm with a mound of salad leaves alongside. Use a mixture of white and brown crab meat if you can: you'll get more crab flavour by using the brown meat too.

SERVES 4

320g (11¼oz) puff pastry sheet

2–3 fresh tarragon sprigs, leaves finely chopped (about 1 tablespoon chopped leaves)

small handful fresh basil leaves, finely chopped

200g (7oz) mixture of white and brown crab meat (or you can just use white)

100ml (3½fl oz) crème fraîche

2 egg yolks

zest of ½ unwaxed lemon

2 tablespoons cress

sea salt and freshly ground black pepper

Preheat your oven to 220°C/425°F/gas mark 7. Line a medium-sized roasting tin with greaseproof paper, then line with your pastry sheet, allowing the pastry to come slightly up the sides of the tin, forming a lip. Prick the pastry well all over and pop into the oven for 12–15 minutes until pale golden.

Meanwhile, in a bowl, mix together the tarragon, basil, crab, crème fraîche, egg yolks and lemon zest; then season.

When the pastry is ready, remove it from the oven. It may have puffed up during that first oven stint; if so, flatten it gently. Spread the crème fraîche mixture over the top of the pastry. Reduce the oven temperature to 160°C/325°F/gas mark 3 and bake for about 15 minutes or until just set and turning golden. Serve warm or at room temperature, topped with the cress.

ALSO WORKS WELL WITH

Flaked hot-smoked trout

Flaked hot-smoked salmon

SPICED TAMARIND & COCONUT PRAWNS
WITH POTATOES

Taking flavour inspiration from southern Indian cuisine, this sweet and spicy dish is delicious as a starter, or served with some rice or bread to make it into more of a main course.

SERVES 2

2 large potatoes (about 500g/1lb 2oz), peeled and cut into roughly 1–2cm (½–¾in) chunks

2 tablespoons coconut oil

4 garlic cloves, thinly sliced

1 red chilli, thinly sliced

1 teaspoon ground coriander

¼ teaspoon ground turmeric

1 teaspoon garam masala

200g (7oz) cherry tomatoes, halved

15 curry leaves

100ml (3½fl oz) coconut milk

1 tablespoon tamarind paste

160g (5¾oz) raw shelled prawns

1 lemon, halved

sea salt and freshly ground black pepper

chopped roasted peanuts, to serve

small handful fresh coriander leaves, to serve

Preheat your oven to 200°C/400°F/gas mark 6. In a medium-sized roasting tin, toss together the potato chunks, coconut oil, garlic, chilli, coriander, turmeric and garam masala with 2 tablespoons of water. Season with salt and lots of black pepper. Roast for 15 minutes, stirring from time to time.

Remove the roasting tin from the oven and add the cherry tomatoes, curry leaves and another 2 tablespoons water. Return to the oven for 5 minutes, then add the coconut milk and tamarind paste. Roast for another 5 minutes, then stir in the prawns and return to the oven for a final 3–5 minutes until the prawns have turned pink.

Squeeze over some lemon juice and sprinkle with some peanuts and coriander before serving.

ALSO WORKS WELL WITH

Firm white fish, such as pollack, pollock, haddock, monkfish or hake, cut into 2.5cm (1in) pieces

Raw scallops

HARISSA & NIGELLA SEED MONKFISH, CLAMS & LENTILS

This recipe is at the more luxurious end of the spectrum, as monkfish and clams are on the dearer side – but, man, they are delicious. I really love the balance of sweet, citrussy, earthy flavours in this recipe; the nigella seeds bring a wonderfully lemony-anise sweetness.

SERVES 4

3 garlic cloves, finely chopped

3 tablespoons olive oil

1 teaspoon nigella seeds

1 teaspoon cumin seeds

pinch of saffron

1 tablespoon rose harissa paste

200g (7oz) roasted red peppers from a jar, drained, rinsed well and roughly chopped

300g (10½oz) tomatoes, finely chopped

450ml (16fl oz) chicken or fish stock

175g (6oz) cavolo nero, any woody stalks removed, shredded

400g (14oz) can beluga lentils (brown or green lentils will also work), drained

400g (14oz) monkfish fillet, cut into 4cm (1½in) chunks

20 clams, prepared according to the instructions on page 16

100g (3½oz) feta cheese

sea salt and freshly ground black pepper

lemon wedges, to serve

Preheat your oven to 220°C/425°F/gas mark 7. Mix together the garlic, oil, nigella seeds, cumin seeds and saffron in a large roasting tin and pop into the oven for 2–3 minutes until the garlic is soft and beginning to take on colour.

Remove the roasting tin from the oven and mix in the harissa, peppers, tomatoes, stock, cavolo nero and lentils. Season, then cover with foil and bake for 7 minutes. Remove the foil and return to the oven for another 10 minutes.

Remove the roasting tin from the oven and tuck the monkfish and clams into the lentil mixture. Return the tin to the oven for a final 6–7 minutes until the monkfish is opaque and the clams have sprung open (discard any that remain closed). Crumble over the feta and serve with lemon wedges for squeezing over.

ALSO WORKS WELL WITH

Any firm white fish, such as haddock, cod, pollock, hake or tilapia

Raw mussels

Raw prawns

BROTHY LEEKS
WITH GIANT COUSCOUS & CLAMS

This dish feels like a fishy version of a magical chicken soup.
As a Jewish gal (not Jewish in a way that means I don't eat
clams or bacon, though), I know the necessity of chicken soup
and the joys that come with it. A restorative and comforting
bowl of food, to warm you inside and out.

SERVES 3

400g (14oz) leeks, trimmed and cut into half
moons

35g (1¼oz) unsalted butter, cut into little
pieces

1 garlic clove, thinly sliced

1 celery stick, chopped

1 carrot, very thinly sliced into quarter moons

5 smoked streaky bacon rashers, finely
chopped

1 fresh bay leaf

80g (2¾oz) giant couscous

100g (3½oz) curly kale or cavolo nero, any
woody stalks removed, chopped

1l (1¾ pints) chicken or fish stock

**21 live clams, prepared according to the
instructions on page 16**

handful fresh flat-leaf parsley, leaves roughly
chopped

zest of 1 unwaxed lemon, plus lemon wedges
to serve

sea salt and freshly ground black pepper

TIP If you want to make this pescatarian,
add a little extra butter at the start of
the recipe, along with a few chopped
canned anchovies for salty savouriness.
You could add a little smoked salt, too,
to emulate the smokiness of the bacon.

Preheat your oven to 230°C/450°F/gas
mark 8. In a medium-sized roasting tin, mix
together the leeks, butter, garlic, celery, carrot,
bacon and bay leaf. Season and cover the
roasting tin with foil. Pop in the oven for
10 minutes, then remove the foil and cook
for a further 5 minutes, or until the vegetables
are soft and starting to colour.

Remove the tin from the oven and add the
couscous and kale or cavolo nero. Pour in
the stock and stir to combine, pushing the
couscous and leaves below the surface of the
stock as much as you can. Reduce the oven
temperature to 200°C/400°F/gas mark 6 and
return the tin to the oven for 10 minutes.

Tuck the clams into the broth and bake for a
further 5 minutes until they've popped open.
Discard any that remain closed. Stir in the
parsley and lemon zest before serving up
with a few lemon wedges alongside.

ALSO WORKS WELL WITH

Live mussels

Raw prawns

Cooked small North Atlantic prawns

WARM BROAD BEAN, CRAB & POTATO SALAD

A jar of dried mint is a wonderful thing to have in your store cupboard: sweet and grassy, with citrus notes, it tastes quite different to its fresh counterpart. Here it sings and prances with sweet and warm flavours, brought to life with the elevating, bright sharpness of lemon.

SERVES 2

350g (12oz) small potatoes, cut into quarters (you want roughly 2.5cm/1in pieces)

2 tablespoons olive oil

¼ teaspoon dried mint, plus extra to serve

generous pinch of pul biber (Aleppo chilli flakes)

2 tablespoons water

1 clementine, zested and halved

200g (7oz) frozen podded broad beans

100g (3½oz) white crab meat

1 unwaxed lemon, zested then halved

small handful fresh dill, roughly chopped

2 tablespoons toasted flaked almonds

sea salt and freshly ground black pepper

Preheat your oven to 220°C/425°F/ gas mark 7. In a medium-sized roasting tin, toss the potatoes with the olive oil, mint, pul biber and measured water. Season, squeeze over the clementine juice and then tuck the clementine halves into the roasting tin, reserving the zest for later. Roast for 20–25 minutes, shaking now and then, until browned and tender.

Meanwhile, steep the broad beans in boiling water to defrost them.

Once the potatoes are soft and burnished, remove the roasting tin from the oven and scoop out the clementine halves. Add the broad beans to the tin, then mix in the crab, clementine zest, lemon zest, a squeeze of lemon juice and dill. Sprinkle with the almonds and some extra mint and serve.

ALSO WORKS WELL WITH

Hot-smoked trout fillets, flesh flaked and skin discarded

Cooked prawns

Brown shrimp

Smoked mackerel fillets, flesh flaked and skin discarded

ANCHOVY, BROCCOLI, CHILLI & GARLIC PASTA

Pasta is one of my all-time favourite foods. It was my breakfast of choice as a stroppy nine-year-old – albeit with sweetcorn and cheese rather than anchovies (those were a little mature for my palate). This is a super-rich, unctuous dish, where the umami qualities of the anchovies really are the star of the show. You can use romanesco or cauliflower in place of broccoli.

SERVES 4

4 tablespoons olive oil

4 garlic cloves, thinly sliced

pinch of chilli flakes

2 rosemary sprigs, leaves stripped and chopped (about ½ tablespoon)

50g (1¾oz) can anchovies, finely chopped, oil reserved

300g (10½oz) dried penne, conchiglie or fusilli pasta

1 chicken stock cube, dissolved in 700ml (1¼ pints) boiling water

400g (14oz) broccoli, broken into small florets, stalk peeled and cut into small chunks

30g (1oz) Parmesan cheese, finely grated, plus extra to serve

sea salt and freshly ground black pepper

TIP Roughly tear two pieces of toast (discarding the crusts; should be about 85g/3oz total weight) and add to the roasting tin at the same time as the oil, garlic, chilli and anchovies. Before you add the pasta and stock, take out the toast and set aside. When you serve the pasta, crumble the toast over the top in crunchy crumbs.

Preheat your oven to 220°C/425°F/gas mark 7. In a large roasting tin, combine the olive oil, garlic, chilli flakes and rosemary with the anchovies and their oil. Pop in the oven for about 5 minutes until the garlic has softened and anchovies have melted.

Remove the roasting tin from the oven and add the dried pasta and stock, then season and cover with foil. Return to the oven for 8 minutes, then remove, peel back the foil and stir in the broccoli. Carefully put the foil back and return the roasting tin to the oven for about 16 minutes. The pasta and broccoli should be tender, and most of the liquid should have been absorbed.

Stir in the cheese, which will emulsify with the liquid remaining in the roasting tin. Serve with lots of extra grated cheese.

ALSO WORKS WELL WITH

Smoked mackerel: flake and stir this in along with the broccoli

SALMON ON TOAST
WITH TAHINI SAUCE

I'm super excited about what is essentially a giant crouton in this dish: just the ticket for soaking up all of the sweet, savoury, earthy flavours. Obviously, you will end up with the best part of a loaf of sourdough left over from this recipe; I often halve the loaf and freeze half for another time, spreading any remaining thickly with butter and jam.

SERVES 2

1 large fennel bulb, any tough outer leaves and core discarded, cut into 8–10 wedges, any fronds reserved

1 tablespoon olive oil, plus extra to drizzle

2 slices of sourdough bread

2 salmon fillets (about 120g/4¼oz each)

sea salt and freshly ground black pepper

FOR THE DRESSING

1 garlic clove, crushed

2 tablespoons tahini

juice of ½ lemon

1–2 tablespoons warm water

Preheat your oven to 220°C/425°F/gas mark 7. In a medium-sized roasting tin, toss the fennel with the olive oil, then season and stir in 3 tablespoons of water. Cover the roasting tin with foil and bake for 20 minutes.

While the fennel cooks, make the dressing. In a small bowl or jug, mix together all the ingredients – you want it to have a drizzle-able consistency.

After 20 minutes, remove the roasting tin from the oven and peel back the foil. Tuck the bread into the roasting tin along with the salmon, skin-side up; drizzle with a little oil and season. Increase the oven temperature to 240°C/475°F/gas mark 9 and return the tin to the oven for 5 minutes, then turn the bread and bake for another 2 minutes, until the salmon flesh flakes easily.

Serve the salmon and fennel atop the toast, drizzled with the tahini dressing, with any reserved fennel fronds sprinkled over the top.

ALSO WORKS WELL WITH

Firm white fish fillets, such as pollack, pollock, cod, haddock or hake

Trout fillets

LEMONY WHOLE TROUT
ATOP STICKY GREEN BEANS & SHALLOTS

When I was little my family often stayed with friends in the Black Mountains. Luke, who was a few years older than me, had a fishing rod and I'd tag along while he fished. I remember him pulling up his line and dangling on the end was a beautifully twinkly rainbow trout. What a prize!

SERVES 2

3 tablespoons olive oil

3 banana shallots, thinly sliced

200g (7oz) fine green beans, topped and tailed

275g (9¾oz) small potatoes, cut into 2mm (¹/₁₆in) slices

1 teaspoon nigella seeds

2 whole rainbow trout (about 250g/9oz each), scaled and gutted

large handful mixed fresh soft herbs, such as dill, parsley, oregano or tarragon

1 teaspoon fennel seeds

zest and juice of 1 unwaxed lemon, plus lemon wedges, to serve

4 tablespoons mayonnaise

4 cornichons, finely chopped

sea salt and freshly ground black pepper

Preheat your oven to 220°C/425°F/gas mark 7. In a large roasting tin, toss together the oil, shallots, green beans, potato slices and nigella seeds. Add 2 tablespoons of water, then season and roast for 10 minutes, stirring from time to time.

Remove the roasting tin from the oven and lie the fish on top of the potatoes and beans, stuffing the cavities with three-quarters of the herbs. Squeeze over the lemon juice, sprinkle over the fennel seeds and season. Pour over an extra 3 tablespoons of water before roasting for a further 15–20 minutes until the fish flesh is opaque and the vegetables tender.

Meanwhile, finely chop the remaining herbs and mix into the mayonnaise, along with the lemon zest and cornichons. Serve the fish with the mayonnaise and lemon wedges.

ALSO WORKS WELL WITH

Whole sea bass

Whole sea bream

Trout fillets (if you cannot get whole trout, you can buy 4 fillets and lie them on top of each other to make 2 mock whole fish)

MACKEREL WITH ROASTED PLUM SAUCE

I feel very excited about this reincarnation of Chinese duck and pancakes. Mackerel is the perfect candidate; the sharp fruit cuts through its rich, oily flesh and skin. These plums are like Chinese plum sauce meets hoisin. The pancakes aren't essential, but they definitely add a certain joy to this dish.

SERVES 4

400g (14oz) plums, stones removed, cut into large chunks

2 tablespoons rice wine vinegar

2 tablespoons soft light brown sugar

2 tablespoons black bean sauce

2 teaspoons sesame oil

25g (1oz) fresh root ginger, finely grated

1 large garlic clove, finely grated

1 star anise

1 hot red chilli, roughly chopped

1½ tablespoons soy sauce

4 mackerel fillets (about 90g/3¼oz each)

sea salt and freshly ground black pepper

TO SERVE (OPTIONAL)

1 pack ready-made Chinese pancakes

1 large spring onion, thinly sliced lengthways

1 small fennel bulb, any tough outer leaves and core discarded, very thinly sliced (or you can use ½ cucumber, very thinly sliced)

Preheat the oven to 220°C/425°F/gas mark 7. In a small roasting tin, combine the plums, vinegar, sugar, black bean sauce, sesame oil, ginger, garlic, star anise, red chilli, soy and 4 tablespoons of water. Roast for 15–20 minutes, stirring now and then, until sticky and burnished.

Once the plums are looking deliciously saucy and sticky, take the roasting tin out of the oven and preheat your grill to high. Give the plums a good stir, breaking them up and making sure to scrape off any bits stuck to the edges of the roasting tin. Have a taste and add more sugar or vinegar if needed.

Lie the mackerel fillets on top of the plums, skin-side up. Season the fish and place under the grill for about 5 minutes until the skin is blistering and the flesh opaque. If serving up with pancakes, prepare according to the packet instructions. Enjoy the fish in chunks, tucked up in a pancake, enveloped in spiced plums with the crunchy veg.

ALSO WORKS WELL WITH

Butterflied sardines: 2–3 per person is perfect (they'll cook quicker, so check them after 3 minutes)

SOUPY CURRIED COCONUT PRAWNS & RICE NOODLES

This soupy dish takes inspiration from laksa and Singapore-style noodles. It's sweet and spicy, salty and savoury. It is also delicious with additional toppings when you want to change things up a little. Have a go mixing and matching with deep-fried tofu, blanched vegetables such as beansprouts or broccoli, slices of raw cucumber or a boiled egg.

SERVES 2

1 aubergine, cut into 2.5cm (1in) chunks

1½ tablespoons sunflower oil

400ml (14fl oz) can coconut milk

300ml (10fl oz) boiling water

1 tablespoon fish sauce

1 tablespoon light soy sauce

100g (3½oz) dried vermicelli rice noodles

200g (7oz) raw shelled prawns

Handful fresh coriander, roughly chopped

sea salt and freshly ground black pepper

lime wedges, to serve

FOR THE CURRY PASTE

½ tablespoon sunflower oil

1 large shallot, roughly chopped

5 garlic cloves, roughly chopped

1 hot Thai red chilli, roughly chopped

½ teaspoon ground turmeric

2 teaspoons mild curry powder

15g (½oz) fresh root ginger, grated

1 lemon grass stalk, tough outer leaves discarded, roughly chopped

Preheat your oven to 220°C/425°F/gas mark 7. First make your curry paste. Using a food processor or stick blender, blitz together all the paste ingredients plus about ½ tablespoon of water to form a fairly smooth mixture.

In a large, deep roasting tin, toss the aubergine with the oil, then season. Roast for about 15 minutes, until starting to colour. Remove the roasting tin from the oven and stir in the spice paste, then return to the oven for another 4–5 minutes.

Remove the roasting tin from the oven and add the coconut milk, measured boiling water, fish sauce, soy sauce and noodles. Push the noodles down into the liquid. Bake for 5 minutes, then tuck the prawns into the mixture and return to the oven for a final 5–6 minutes until the prawns are pink and the noodles tender. Garnish with the coriander and serve with a wedge of lime.

ALSO WORKS WELL WITH

6cm (2½in) chunks of firm white fish such as haddock, cod, pollock or hake (these might need slightly longer to cook, so add them when you add the noodles)

Live clams

Live mussels

HERBY PEA & CRAB GNOCCHI

You can use fresh or canned crab for this recipe. If you use canned, try to get lump or jumbo: they have a better flavour and texture than shredded. If you are using fresh crab, a mixture of brown and white crab meat brings an extra depth of crabby flavour. Tarragon can be a divisive herb, but I love its sweet anise flavour. A little goes a long way, so on the whole use sparingly.

SERVES 4

200g (7oz) frozen petit pois

250g (9oz) mascarpone cheese

200ml (7fl oz) milk

zest of 1 unwaxed lemon

3 sprigs tarragon, leaves finely chopped

small handful fresh dill, leaves finely chopped

handful fresh basil, leaves finely chopped

3 spring onions, finely sliced

2 garlic cloves, crushed

35g (1¼ oz) Parmesan cheese, grated

500g (1lb 2oz) gnocchi

200g (7oz) mixture of white and brown crab meat (or you can just use white)

sea salt and freshly ground black pepper

Preheat your oven to 220°C/425°F/gas mark 7. Pop the peas into a measuring jug and cover them with boiling water. Leave to stand for about 5 minutes until the peas are defrosted, then drain and return them to the jug.

Spoon the mascarpone into the jug along with the milk, then blend until smooth using a stick blender. Mix in the lemon zest, herbs, spring onions, garlic and about half of the cheese; then season.

Place the gnocchi in a small roasting tin, then mix in the pea sauce and crab. Sprinkle the remaining cheese over the top and bake for 20 minutes until looking golden and bubbly. It will be fairly runny at this point, so leave it to stand for 5 minutes before serving; it continues to thicken as it stands.

ALSO WORKS WELL WITH

Raw prawns

Brown shrimp

Hot-smoked salmon fillets, flesh flaked and skin discarded

ZA'ATAR-RUBBED MACKEREL ON MIXED PEPPERS & FREEKEH

This dish is perfect for long summer evenings. Set up your dinner table outside, make a large leafy salad and get the rosé flowing. Za'atar is a spice-and-herb mix originating in the Middle East, usually made up of thyme, marjoram, oregano, sesame seeds and often sumac. The balance of flavours will vary quite a bit depending on where you buy it. You might want to add more or less than I've suggested, so just adjust to your taste.

SERVES 4

2 red, orange or yellow peppers, cut into thick strips

1 green pepper, cut into thick strips

2 tablespoons olive oil, plus extra to drizzle

3 garlic cloves, bashed, skin left on

2 red onions, cut into slim wedges

4 whole mackerel (about 300g/10½oz each), scaled and gutted

small handful fresh coriander, sprigs left whole

small handful fresh flat-leaf parsley, sprigs left whole

4 wide strips unwaxed orange zest

4 wide strips unwaxed lemon zest, plus lemon wedges, to serve

250g (9oz) pouch cooked freekeh

1½ teaspoons za'atar

sea salt and freshly ground black pepper

plain yogurt, to serve

Preheat your oven to 240°C/475°F/gas mark 9. In a large roasting tin, toss together the peppers, olive oil, garlic and red onions. Season, then roast for 10 minutes.

Meanwhile, stuff the fish with the herbs and strips of zest.

Remove the roasting tin from the oven and stir the freekeh into the peppers, then place the mackerel on top. Drizzle with a little extra oil. Reduce the oven temperature to 220°C/425°F/gas mark 7 and pop the tin back into the oven for 15–17 minutes until the fish flesh is opaque. Sprinkle with the za'atar and enjoy with a good dollop of yogurt and lemon wedges for squeezing.

ALSO WORKS WELL WITH

Whole sardines (you will need 8–12; cook the peppers for about 15–17 minutes before adding the fish for a final 10–15 minutes)

Whole rainbow trout

Whole sea bream

READY IN 45 MINUTES

PANKO-CRUSTED COD
WITH STICKY GOCHUJANG CABBAGE

A few years ago, I was lucky enough to work on the brilliant Korean cookbook *K Food* by Da-Hae West and Gareth West. I had never really eaten or cooked much Korean food before, and it was a delicious, eye-opening experience. Gochujang is used heavily throughout Korean cooking. It is a wonderfully sweet, savoury, spicy fermented paste.

SERVES 2

½ large white cabbage (about 700g/1lb 9oz), any tough core removed, shredded

2 tablespoons sunflower oil, plus extra for drizzling

3 tablespoons gochujang

3 garlic cloves, crushed

2 tablespoons cider vinegar

2 tablespoons soy sauce

pinch of caster or granulated sugar

bunch of spring onions, 2 thinly sliced and the rest roughly chopped

7 tablespoons panko breadcrumbs

3 tablespoons plain flour

1 medium egg, beaten

2 thick cod fillets (about 150g/5½oz each), skin removed

sea salt and freshly ground black pepper

sesame oil, to serve

Preheat the oven to 230°C/450°F/gas mark 8. In a large, ideally non-stick, roasting tin, toss the cabbage with the oil, gochujang, garlic, cider vinegar, soy sauce, sugar, roughly chopped spring onions and 3 tablespoons of water. Roast for 15–20 minutes, stirring now and then, until the cabbage is tender and starting to look burnished.

While the cabbage is cooking, prepare the fish. Put the breadcrumbs into one bowl, the flour into another and the egg into a third. Season the flour with salt and black pepper. Dip each fish fillet into the flour, then the egg and finally coat in breadcrumbs.

Remove the roasting tin from the oven and make two spaces in the cabbage. Pop the fish into the spaces you've created and drizzle with a little oil. Bake for 7 minutes, then turn the fish over and bake for another 6–7 minutes. The breadcrumb coating should be turning golden and when investigated the flesh firm and opaque. Sprinkle over the thinly sliced spring onion and drizzle with a little sesame oil.

ALSO WORKS WELL WITH

Firm white fish fillets, such as pollack, pollock, haddock, monkfish or hake

FISH & PRAWN GRATIN
WITH A CHEESY CRUMB TOPPING

This is like an extra cheesy and indulgent fish pie: a warming dish for chilly nights. Serve up with some steamed greens, and get cosy in front of a log burner (real or TV version – both work here).

SERVES 4

3 leeks, trimmed and sliced into rounds

2 fresh bay leaves

60g (2¼oz) unsalted butter, cut into little pieces

250g (9oz) baby spinach

300ml (10fl oz) double cream

handful fresh flat-leaf parsley, leaves finely chopped

zest of 1 unwaxed lemon

115g (4oz) Gruyère cheese, coarsely grated

2 egg yolks

500g (1lb 2oz) fish pie mix (or see Tip)

150g (5½oz) raw shelled prawns

75g (2¾oz) panko breadcrumbs

olive oil, to drizzle

sea salt and freshly ground black pepper

Preheat your oven to 200°C/400°F/gas mark 6. Add the leeks, bay leaves and butter to a small roasting tin. Season, then cover with tin foil and pop in the oven for 20 minutes.

Meanwhile, put the spinach into a colander and pour over a kettleful of boiling water. Squeeze out any excess water using a wooden spoon.

After 20 minutes, take the roasting tin out of the oven and stir in the wilted spinach, along with the cream, parsley, lemon zest, 50g (1¾oz) of the Gruyère and the egg yolks. Tuck the fish and prawns into the cream mixture, then sprinkle over the breadcrumbs and remaining cheese. Drizzle with olive oil and return to the oven for 25 minutes until golden and bubbling.

ALSO WORKS WELL WITH

Swap the prawns for brown shrimp

TIPS Make up your own fish pie mix with smoked haddock, a firm white fish and some salmon.
For something a little less rich, replace some of the cream with full-fat crème fraîche.

BRAISED SQUID & CHICKPEAS

Squid needs a quick, hot treatment or a slow, cool one.
This recipe shows you how to prepare the latter. The result
is tender, meaty squid in a rich, soupy stew. Feel free to wilt
in some chard or spinach towards the end of cooking.

SERVES 2

1 large onion, finely chopped

pinch of chilli flakes

pinch of fennel seeds

4 tablespoons olive oil

1 fresh bay leaf

4 large sage leaves, finely chopped

2 garlic cloves, sliced

**2 whole squid (about 350g/12oz total
weight), cleaned and cut into thick rings,
tentacles separated from the body and
kept whole**

400g (14oz) can plum tomatoes

400ml (14fl oz) chicken stock

100ml (3½fl oz) sherry

1 tablespoon red wine vinegar

400g (14oz) can chickpeas, drained

small handful fresh dill, leaves picked

sea salt and freshly ground black pepper

lemon wedges, to serve

Preheat your oven to 220°C/425°F/gas mark
7. In a medium-sized roasting tin, combine
the onion, chilli flakes, fennel seeds, olive
oil, bay, sage and garlic. Pop into the oven for
about 5 minutes, or until the onion and garlic
are tender.

Remove the roasting tin from the oven and stir
in the squid, tomatoes, stock, sherry, vinegar
and chickpeas; then season. Reduce the oven
temperature to 140°C/280°F/gas mark 1 and
bake for 40 minutes. The sauce should have
thickened a little, and the squid should be
tender. Stir in the dill and serve with a wedge
of lemon.

ALSO WORKS WELL WITH

Cuttlefish

A nice 400g (14oz) piece of firm white fish,
such as monkfish or haddock (this will need
less cooking, so add it about 15–20 minutes
before the end)

JERK SALMON
WITH RICE & PEAS

I grew up in Brixton, where delicious Caribbean food smells wafted down the street, making my tummy rumble and drawing me in for a post-school patty. Thank you to my pals Rio and Esther for being a sounding board on this recipe.

SERVES 4

4 salmon fillets, skin removed (about 120g/4¼oz each)

2 red peppers, cut into strips

1 scotch bonnet chilli, halved but still attached at the stalk

1 large onion, roughly chopped

6 thyme sprigs

2 garlic cloves, thinly sliced

2 tablespoons coconut oil

250g (9oz) white basmati rice

400g (14oz) can kidney beans, drained and rinsed

400ml (14fl oz) can coconut milk

250ml (9fl oz) boiling water

sea salt and freshly ground black pepper

lemon wedges, to serve

coleslaw, to serve

FOR THE JERK SEASONING

145g (5¼oz) spring onions

3 garlic cloves

20g (¾oz) fresh root ginger, roughly chopped

2 teaspoons ground allspice

1 teaspoon each ground nutmeg and ground cinnamon

1 scotch bonnet pepper, halved

3½ tablespoons light soy sauce

4½ tablespoons cider vinegar

1 tablespoon each fresh thyme leaves and dark soft brown sugar

pinch of sea salt and ½ teaspoon freshly ground black pepper

Use a stick blender to blitz together the jerk seasoning ingredients. You want a fine, fairly runny paste. This recipe will make double, so freeze the other half. Place the salmon in a shallow dish or bowl and rub with 6 tablespoons of the jerk seasoning. Set aside to marinate. If you have time, leave your salmon to marinate in the fridge, covered, for a few hours before cooking.

Preheat the oven to 240°C/475°F/gas mark 9. In a large roasting tin, toss together the peppers, chilli, onion, thyme, garlic and coconut oil. Pop into the oven for 10–12 minutes, stirring once or twice, until the onion and peppers are soft and starting to catch in places, turning a golden brown.

Remove the roasting tin from the oven and stir in the rice, kidney beans, coconut milk and measured boiling water. Season and cover the roasting tin with foil. Reduce the oven temperature to 220°C/425°F/gas mark 7 and bake for 20 minutes.

Remove the roasting tin from the oven once again. Stir the rice mixture, then tuck in the salmon, drizzling over any excess jerk marinade. Replace the foil and pop back in the oven for 10–12 minutes until the fish flakes easily. Serve with lemon wedges, for squeezing, and coleslaw.

ALSO WORKS WELL WITH
Trout fillets

Mackerel fillets

STEWED CHICKPEAS & SPINACH
WITH SMOKED HADDOCK

This is inspired by a dish that is on pretty much every tapas menu in Seville: espinacas con garbanzos. Traditionally, there is no fish in this dish, but I feel the smoked haddock brings a wonderfully savoury note. I love this dish. So hassle-free, it's perfect for autumnal days when the nights are closing in. Add a few chilli flakes if you like a little heat.

SERVES 4

6 tablespoons olive oil, plus extra to serve

4 garlic cloves, thinly sliced

2 teaspoons cumin seeds

1 teaspoon sweet smoked paprika, plus extra to serve

450g (1lb) baby spinach, chopped (I use scissors to snip the leaves in their bag)

2 x 400g (14oz) cans chickpeas, 1 drained

4–5 large tomatoes (about 450g/1lb), deseeded and roughly chopped

340g (12oz) skinless smoked haddock (about 3 fillets)

1 tablespoon sherry vinegar

sea salt and freshly ground black pepper

Preheat your oven to 220°C/425°F/gas mark 7. Add the oil, garlic and cumin seeds to a large roasting tin. Pop into the oven for 5 minutes until the garlic is soft and smells fragrant.

Add the paprika, spinach, chickpeas (including the liquid from 1 can) and tomatoes. Season, add 3 tablespoons of water, cover with foil and bake for 20 minutes.

After 20 minutes, remove the foil and bake for another 10 minutes.

Remove the roasting tin from the oven. Crush one side of the contents (about half) with a potato masher, then stir together to combine the crushed and not-crushed parts. Tuck the fish into the stew and bake for a further 10 minutes, or until the fish is opaque. Stir in the vinegar and break the fish into chunks. Sprinkle over some extra paprika and serve with a glug of olive oil.

ALSO WORKS WELL WITH

Smoked cod fillets

FISH BALLS POACHED IN A ROASTED TOMATO SAUCE

Lighter than a meatball, but just as satisfying, these fish balls are delicious piled up on buttery couscous or stirred through pasta.

SERVES 4

3 garlic cloves, sliced

¼ teaspoon ground cinnamon

2 tablespoons olive oil

1 teaspoon rose harissa paste

pinch of caster or granulated sugar

2 x 400g (14oz) cans chopped tomatoes

sea salt and freshly ground black pepper

FOR THE FISH BALLS

500g (1lb 2oz) skinless pollock, finely chopped or minced

4 tablespoons dried breadcrumbs (such as panko)

1 medium egg, beaten

pinch of ground nutmeg

zest of 1 unwaxed lemon

1 garlic clove, crushed

handful fresh flat-leaf parsley, leaves finely chopped

TO SERVE

small handful fresh dill, leaves picked

grated Parmesan cheese

bread or toast

lemon wedges

Preheat the oven to 200°C/400°F/gas mark 6. In a medium-sized roasting tin, mix together the garlic, cinnamon and olive oil. Pop in the oven for 4–5 minutes until the garlic is soft – be careful not to let it catch and burn.

Remove the roasting tin from the oven and stir in the harissa, sugar and tomatoes, then season and return to the oven for 15 minutes.

Meanwhile, make up the little fish balls. In a large bowl, combine the fish, breadcrumbs, egg, nutmeg, lemon zest, garlic and parsley. Season well and mix thoroughly with your hands, then shape the mixture into walnut-sized balls (about 15–20) and set aside.

After 15 minutes, remove the roasting tin from the oven and tuck the fish balls into the tomato sauce. Splash over 3 tablespoons of water, then cover the tin with foil and bake for 20 another minutes or until the fish is opaque.

To serve, sprinkle the dish with the dill and a generous amount of Parmesan. Have some bread or toast alongside for scooping, and a lemon wedge for squeezing.

ALSO WORKS WELL WITH

Any firm white fish, such as haddock, cod, hake or tilapia

SMOKY RICE
WITH PRAWN & CHORIZO

This is my version of a jambalaya. Jambalaya originated in Louisiana; it was a one-pot dish, made from things that were easy to come by. The dish differs from family to family and neighbourhood to neighbourhood, but there are two distinctive approaches: Cajun and Creole. Cajun jambalaya focuses on smoked meats, while the Creole version has the addition of tomatoes and seafood. This recipe is closer to the Creole dish.

SERVES 4

6 smoked streaky bacon rashers, cut into little pieces

2 cooking chorizo sausages (about 140g/5oz), cut into little pieces

1 large onion, chopped

1 green pepper, chopped

2 celery sticks, chopped

1 fresh bay leaf

3 garlic cloves, finely chopped

2 tablespoons sunflower oil

1 teaspoon dried thyme

1 teaspoon paprika

½ teaspoon cayenne pepper

250g (9oz) long grain rice

1 fish stock cube, dissolved in 600ml (20fl oz) boiling water

400g (14oz) can plum tomatoes

225g (8oz) raw shelled prawns

sea salt and freshly ground black pepper

lemon wedges, to serve

chopped spring onions, to serve (optional)

Preheat your oven to 240°C/475°F/gas mark 9. In a large roasting tin, mix together the bacon, chorizo, onion, green pepper, celery, bay, garlic and oil. Roast for about 10–15 minutes, tossing from time to time, until everything has started to take on a little colour and the vegetables are tender.

Remove the roasting tin from the oven and stir in the thyme, paprika, cayenne, rice, stock and tomatoes, breaking up the tomatoes with the spoon as you stir them in. Season and cover the roasting tin with foil. Bake for 20 minutes.

Remove the roasting tin from the oven and peel back the foil. Fluff up the rice with a fork, then tuck the prawns in and replace the foil. Turn off the oven and pop the roasting tin back in for 7 minutes. The prawns will cook in the residual heat. Serve with lemon wedges and sprinkled with chopped spring onions, if you like!

TIPS You can be a bit flexible about what kind of sausage and bacon you use, as long as there is some smokiness going on.
If you want to make this pescatarian, use some monkfish in place of the meat and pop in some extra paprika and smoked salt to make up for the lack of smoked bacon and sausage.

HOT-SMOKED SALMON
WITH HONEYED CARAWAY CARROTS & BITTER LEAVES

This rich, smoky salmon is delicious paired with the sweet and earthy carrots. If you like, you could replace the carrots with another sweet root, such as beetroot or parsnip. Equally, you could try this with potatoes or sweet potatoes.

SERVES 2

2 tablespoons olive oil

4 large carrots, cut into chunks

2 red onions, cut into slender wedges

2 teaspoons runny honey

1 teaspoon caraway seeds

2 teaspoons wholegrain mustard

2 hot-smoked salmon fillets (about 100g/3½oz each)

2 heads of chicory, leaves separated and any large ones torn

sea salt and freshly ground black pepper

Preheat your oven to 220°C/425°F/gas mark 7. In a small roasting tin, mix together the olive oil, carrots, onions, honey, caraway seeds and mustard; then season. Roast for 35 minutes, stirring now and then until tender and browning.

Remove from the oven and add the salmon to the roasting tin, then roast for a further 5 minutes.

To serve, flake the fish into the roasting tin, discarding the skin, and fold through the chicory.

ALSO WORKS WELL WITH

Hot-smoked trout fillets

Hot-smoked mackerel fillets

Salmon fillets (these will need longer to cook – more like 8–12 minutes)

BROTHY LAYERS OF POTATO
WITH SEA BASS & AIOLI

This über-simple dish is really shining a spotlight on the delicious and (in my view) under-celebrated potato. Here, potato slices cook slowly in the stock, resulting in unctuously soft and sweet potato dreaminess. The sea bass is left unadulterated as the jewel in the crown, so try to buy the best fish you can. The aioli recipe makes more than you need for this dish, so transfer any extra to a tub and keep in the refrigerator for spreading thickly on bread later.

SERVES 2

400g (14oz) Maris Piper or King Edward potatoes or other floury potato, peeled and cut into 5mm (¼in) slices

2 tablespoons olive oil, plus extra to drizzle

2 fresh bay leaves

250g (9oz) large tomatoes, cut into slim slices

350ml (12fl oz) chicken or fish stock

1 whole sea bass (about 700g/1lb 9oz), scaled and gutted

sea salt and freshly ground black pepper

FOR THE AIOLI

1 egg yolk

1 teaspoon cider vinegar

zest of 1 unwaxed lemon, plus lemon wedges, to serve

1 large garlic clove, crushed or finely grated

200ml (7fl oz) mild olive oil

Preheat your oven to 220°C/425°F/gas mark 7. In a large roasting tin, toss the potato slices with the olive oil, season and tuck in the bay leaves. Roast for 10 minutes until starting to turn golden.

Remove the roasting tin from the oven and add the slices of tomato, tucking them in between pieces of potato. Pour over the stock and arrange the fish on top. Season the fish inside and out, then drizzle it with a little olive oil. Reduce the oven temperature to 200°C/400°F/gas mark 6. Bake for about 15–20 minutes, until the fish feels firm and, when poked with the tip of a knife, comes away from the bones.

While the fish cooks, make the aioli. In a bowl, beat the egg yolk with the cider vinegar, lemon zest and garlic. Put the oil into a jug and very slowly pour it into the bowl, whisking all the time. Only add more oil once the previous oil has been fully incorporated and emulsified. Continue this process until all the oil has been added: it should look like a lovely, wobbly mayo! Check the seasoning and add a little lemon juice if you fancy.

Serve the soft and sticky potatoes and fish with the aioli and some lemon wedges to squeeze over.

ALSO WORKS WELL WITH

You can use two smaller sea bass for this recipe – just check whether they're cooked a little earlier

Whole sea bream

WHOLE SEA BASS
WITH GINGER, SICHUAN PEPPER & CELERY

Having explored a multitude of Chinese jarred chilli oils, black bean is my absolute favourite. It's sweet, spicy and salty: drizzle it on most things for instant meal gratification. This baked sea bass takes loose flavour inspiration from the iconic Sichuan dish, gong bao chicken.

SERVES 2

1 teaspoon Sichuan peppercorns

2 sticks celery, thinly sliced

2 tablespoons sunflower oil

125g (4½oz) jasmine rice

300ml (10fl oz) chicken or fish stock

2 whole sea bass (about 350g/12oz each), scaled and gutted

2 spring onions, halved widthways

2 garlic cloves, thinly sliced

15g (½oz) fresh root ginger, thinly sliced

2 tablespoons Shaoxing wine

1½ teaspoons sesame oil

4 teaspoons light soy sauce

1 tablespoon black bean chilli oil (I like the Lao Gan Ma brand)

sea salt

Preheat your oven to 220°C/425°F/gas mark 7. Add the Sichuan peppercorns to a large roasting tin and place in the hot oven for about 3–5 minutes until they release their aroma.

Remove the roasting tin from the oven. Tip out the peppercorns and finely chop them, then return them to the roasting tin, along with the celery and sunflower oil. Return the tin to the oven for 10 minutes, by which point the celery should be softening and taking on some colour.

Remove the roasting tin from the oven and stir the rice into the celery, along with the stock. Season with salt. Lie the sea bass on top of the rice-and-celery mixture and cut three slashes in each fish. Stuff their bellies with the spring onions and the slashes with the garlic and ginger, then season inside and out with salt. Pour the Shaoxing over the fish, then cover the roasting tin with foil, leaving a nice tent-like space above the fish. Reduce the oven temperature to 200°C/400°F/gas mark 6 and bake for about 20–25 minutes. The fish should feel firm and, when investigated with the point of a knife, should peel away from the bones easily. If it isn't there yet, just re-cover with the foil and pop back into the oven for a couple of minutes.

When it's ready, drizzle over the sesame oil, soy sauce and black bean chilli oil, and serve.

ALSO WORKS WELL WITH
Whole sea bream
Whole trout

SMOKED HADDOCK DAHL
WITH COCONUT, CURRY LEAVES & TOMATOES

I find the combination of smoked fish and spices so comforting. My granny often cooked up a big pan of kedgeree when we went over at the weekend, covered in boiled eggs – which, at the time, I fussed over, as boiled eggs were (and really still are) my nemesis. This dahl would be delicious served up with a crisp-bottomed fried egg – or even a runny boiled one, if that takes your fancy.

SERVES 4

2½ tablespoons coconut oil

1 teaspoon brown mustard seeds

1 teaspoon fenugreek seeds

1 teaspoon cumin seeds

2 small chillies, finely chopped

4 garlic cloves, sliced

20 curry leaves

2 red onions, finely sliced

1kg (2lb 4oz) large tomatoes, each cut into 6 wedges

200g (7oz) dried red lentils

400ml (14fl oz) can coconut milk

200ml (7fl oz) boiling water

340g (12oz) skinless smoked haddock (about 3 fillets), cut into 3cm (1¼in) pieces

1 lemon, halved

small handful fresh coriander leaves

sea salt and freshly ground black pepper

chapati or toast, to serve

Preheat your oven to 220°C/425°F/gas mark 7. In a large roasting tin, combine the coconut oil, mustard seeds, fenugreek, cumin seeds, chillies, garlic, curry leaves and onions. Season and pop in the oven for 6 minutes, stirring now and then.

Remove the roasting tin from the oven, stir in the tomatoes and roast for a further 9 minutes.

Remove the roasting tin from the oven once again and mix in the lentils, coconut milk and measured boiling water. Return to the oven and bake for 25 minutes.

Remove from the oven once more and tuck in the fish pieces. Return to the oven and cook for a final 5–6 minutes until the fish is opaque. Squeeze over a little lemon juice and sprinkle with the coriander. Serve with some chapati or toast.

ALSO WORKS WELL WITH

Raw prawns

Smoked cod fillets

Firm white fish fillets, such as pollack, pollock, haddock, tilapia or hake

ROAST HAKE
WITH BLACK LENTILS, SQUASH & CHILLI SAUCE

The chilli sauce in this dish is based on the Levantine condiment shatta (which literally translates from the Arabic as 'hot sauce'). This recipe makes more than you'll need, so pop the rest into a clean jar and keep in the refrigerator to enjoy over the next few weeks. My friend John likes to spread some beneath a good Cheddar for a seriously lush cheese on toast.

SERVES 2

700g (1lb 9oz) butternut squash or pumpkin, peeled, halved, seeds scooped out and cut into slim slices

2 tablespoons olive oil, plus extra to drizzle

½ teaspoon ground cumin

¼ teaspoon ground cinnamon

250g (9oz) pouch beluga lentils (Puy, brown or green lentils will also work)

2 hake fillets (about 120g/4¼oz each)

small handful fresh dill, leaves picked

sea salt and freshly ground black pepper

plain yogurt, to serve

FOR THE CHILLI SAUCE

120g (4¼oz) large fresh red chillies, roughly chopped (if you want it a little less spicy, remove the seeds)

2 garlic cloves, roughly chopped

2 tablespoons olive oil

1 teaspoon caraway seeds

¾ teaspoon ground coriander

juice of ½ lemon

Preheat your oven to 220°C/425°F/gas mark 7. In a large roasting tin, toss together the squash or pumpkin, olive oil, cumin and cinnamon. Season and roast for 25–30 minutes, turning from time to time, until tender and burnished.

While the squash cooks, make the chilli sauce. Using a stick blender, blitz together the chillies, garlic, olive oil, caraway, coriander and lemon juice. Season to taste and set aside.

After 25–30 minutes, remove the roasting tin from the oven and mix in the lentils. Arrange the fish on top skin-side down, then season and drizzle with a little oil. Pop back into the oven for about 6–8 minutes until the fish flesh is opaque and flakes easily.

To serve, sprinkle over the dill, spoon over some of the chilli sauce and tuck in with a dollop of yogurt on the side.

ALSO WORKS WELL WITH

Firm white fish fillets, such as pollack, pollock, cod or haddock

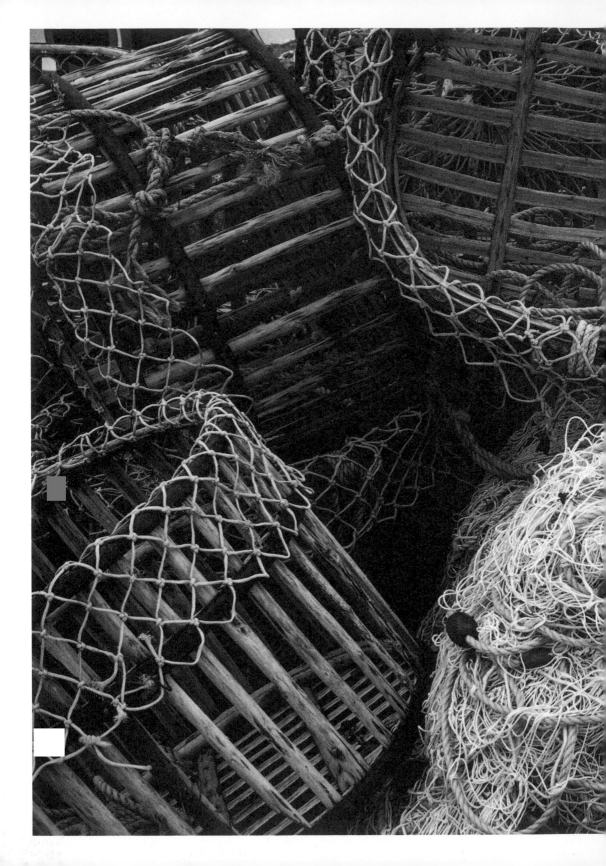

SALMON & PEA PILAF
WITH BROWN BUTTER & FENUGREEK

Perfect cosy fare: nutty brown butter is one of life's great pleasures. As well as being delicious in this dish, try it poured it over pasta or mashed it into potatoes, or use in pancakes or muffins for added depth and richness. You can use garden peas or broad beans in place of petits pois, but they'll be less sweet. I love the little pops of sweetness you get from these tiny peas.

SERVES 4

35g (1¼oz) unsalted butter

1 tablespoon sunflower oil

2 onions, chopped

1 small garlic clove, thinly sliced

1 cardamom pod, bashed

2 cloves

1 teaspoon fenugreek

250g (9oz) white basmati rice

200g (7oz) petit pois

600ml (20fl oz) boiling water

2 salmon fillets (about 120g/4¼oz each), skin removed, cut into 2.5cm (1in) chunks

sea salt and freshly ground black pepper

FOR THE YOGURT SAUCE

handful fresh coriander, leaves picked

2 fresh mint sprigs, leaves picked

small handful fresh dill, leaves picked

1 small green chilli, finely chopped

1 small garlic clove, sliced

3 tablespoons plain yogurt

juice of ½ a small lemon

Preheat your oven to 220°C/425°F/gas mark 7. Place the butter in a small roasting tin and put it in the oven for 1 minute, then give it a shake and return it to the oven for another 1–3 minutes. Check it after every minute: it should be melted, smell nutty and have dark golden flecks in it.

Pour the sunflower oil into the roasting tin and add the onions, the garlic clove, and the cardamom, cloves and fenugreek. Return the tin to the oven for 10–15 minutes until the onions and garlic are soft and tinged golden.

Remove the roasting tin from the oven and stir in the rice, peas and measured boiling water. Season, then cover with foil and bake for 20 minutes.

Meanwhile, make the yogurt sauce. Place all the ingredients in a bowl or jug and use a stick blender to blitz them together.

After 20 minutes, remove the roasting tin from the oven. Peel back the foil and tuck in the salmon among the rice and peas. Put back the foil cover and return the tin to the oven for a final 5 minutes until the fish is an opaque, light pink and flakes easily. Serve with the yogurt sauce.

ALSO WORKS WELL WITH

Trout fillets

Smoked haddock fillets

MACKEREL ON TURNIPS
WITH SMOKED BACON & FENNEL SEEDS

Turnips are something that deserve some more appreciation. My favourite way to eat them is caramelised in butter and braised in stock; they are absolutely delicious. Here, their earthy sweetness works wonderfully with the mackerel. Please, fall in love with turnips.

SERVES 2

200g (7oz) new potatoes, sliced into slim rounds

3 small turnips (about 225g/8oz), peeled, halved and cut into slim rounds

6 smoked streaky bacon rashers, cut into small pieces

½ teaspoon fennel seeds

35g (1¼oz) unsalted butter, cut into little pieces

pinch of caster or granulated sugar

450ml (16fl oz) chicken or fish stock

2 whole mackerel (about 300g/10½oz each), scaled and gutted

6 tarragon sprigs

½ lemon, sliced

sea salt and freshly ground black pepper

Preheat your oven to 220°C/425°F/gas mark 7. In a large roasting tin, toss together the potatoes and turnips with the bacon, fennel seeds, butter and sugar. Roast for 10–15 minutes, tossing from time to time, until taking on some colour.

Remove the roasting tin from the oven and pour in the stock, then return to the oven for another 10–15 minutes.

Remove the roasting tin from the oven once more and lie the mackerel on top of the potato mixture. Stuff the fish cavities with the tarragon and lemon slices, then season the fish inside and out with salt and black pepper. Return to the oven and bake for about 12–15 minutes, or until the flesh feels firm and peels away from the bones easily when poked with a knife. Serve.

ALSO WORKS WELL WITH

Mackerel fillets (you can buy 4 fillets and lie them on top of each other to make 2 mock whole fish if you cannot get whole mackerel)

Whole trout

TIP If you want to make this pescatarian, add a little extra butter at the start of the recipe and a few chopped canned anchovies for salty savouriness. You could add a pinch of smoked salt to emulate the smokiness of the bacon.

MONKFISH TAGINE

This stew is an unctuous embodiment of autumn, with warm spices and beautiful tones of gold and green. The firm and meaty fish holds its shape in a slow stew and works wonderfully with the sweet and sour flavours. Try toasting some blanched almonds, then chopping to scatter over the top as a finishing touch. If you don't have an apple or prunes, you can try using a pear or raisins instead.

SERVES 4

1 large onion, chopped

3 garlic cloves, finely chopped

60g (2¼oz) unsalted butter

large handful fresh coriander, stalks and leaves roughly chopped

2 teaspoons ground ginger

pinch of saffron

1 cinnamon stick

1½ preserved lemons (about 35g/1¼oz), flesh discarded, finely chopped

100ml (3½fl oz) fish stock

1 apple, peeled, cored and cut into small pieces (roughly 1.5cm/⅝in)

400g (14oz) can chickpeas, drained

40g (1½oz) prunes, roughly chopped

250g (9oz) chard or spinach (baby spinach can be used but large leaf spinach is best), washed and chopped

600g (1lb 5oz) piece monkfish fillet, cut into 6cm (2½in) chunks

sea salt and freshly ground black pepper

bread or couscous, to serve

Preheat your oven to 220°C/425°F/gas mark 7. Pop the onion and garlic into a medium-sized roasting tin, dot over the butter and slip into the oven for about 10 minutes, stirring once or twice, until the onion and garlic are softening and turning golden at the edges.

Remove the roasting tin from the oven and mix in the coriander, ginger, saffron and cinnamon stick. Return to the oven for about 3 minutes, then remove once again and stir in the preserved lemons, stock, apple, chickpeas and prunes. Season and bake for 15 minutes.

Remove the roasting tin from the oven and stir in the chard or spinach and monkfish, then cover with foil. Reduce the oven temperature to 180°C/350°F/gas mark 4 and return the tin to the oven for a final 10–12 minutes. When it's ready, the chard or spinach will have wilted and made the tagine nice and saucy, and the fish should be opaque. Serve with bread or buttery couscous.

ALSO WORKS WELL WITH

Any firm white fish, such as haddock, cod, pollock or hake

CREAMY COD, PRAWN & GNOCCHI BAKE
WITH SWEET ONIONS

This dish takes inspiration from the delicious Swedish dish Jansson's temptation, which is a gratin of sorts: layers of potato, canned sprats and onions baked in cream. I love the sweet, sour, creamy combination. Do a little jar investigation when shopping and try to get cornichons that have a higher sugar content.

SERVES 4

2 onions, thinly sliced

35g (1¼oz) unsalted butter, cut into small pieces

2 tablespoons olive oil

generous pinch of ground cinnamon

generous pinch of ground allspice

1 fresh bay leaf

500g (1lb 2oz) gnocchi

150g (5½oz) cooked small North Atlantic prawns

250g (9oz) smoked cod, skin removed, cut into 2.5cm (1in) chunks

7 cornichons, finely chopped, plus 3 tablespoons of the pickling liquid, and extra for drizzling (optional)

200ml (7fl oz) double cream

200ml (7fl oz) full-fat crème fraîche

150ml (5fl oz) milk

4 tablespoons dried breadcrumbs (such as panko)

sea salt and freshly ground black pepper

Preheat your oven to 220°C/425°F/gas mark 7. In a small roasting tin, toss together the onions, butter, oil, cinnamon, allspice and bay leaf. Season with salt and pop into the oven for 15–20 minutes, stirring from time to time, until the onions are soft and beginning to go brown.

Remove the roasting tin from the oven and mix in the gnocchi, prawns, cod, cornichons, pickling liquid, cream, crème fraîche and milk. Top with the breadcrumbs. Reduce the oven temperature to 200°C/400°F/gas mark 6 and bake for 15 minutes until turning golden and bubbling round the edges. Serve with a good grinding of black pepper and a drizzle of extra pickle juice, if you fancy.

ALSO WORKS WELL WITH

Smoked haddock fillets

Cooked large prawns

Brown shrimp

LENTILS & RICE
WITH SMOKED MACKEREL & STICKY ONIONS

This dish is similar to one I have shared many times with my
Aunty Sarah. It's always a little different: sometimes tomatoes,
sometimes onions; maybe served with yogurt or grated cheese.
The constant is lentils and rice, an ever-satisfying duo.

SERVES 3

2 tablespoons ghee or butter

**2 x 110g (3¾oz) cans smoked mackerel,
oil reserved**

2 onions, thinly sliced

1 green chilli, finely chopped

1 fresh bay leaf

2 teaspoons mild curry powder

2 cardamom pods

400g (14oz) can green lentils, drained

125g (4½oz) white basmati rice

300ml (10fl oz) boiling water

sea salt

plain yogurt, to serve

sliced cucumber and tomato, to serve
(optional)

TIP Try frying some eggs to top this
dish. Heat 1 tablespoon ghee in a
frying pan. Once hot, add ½ teaspoon
mustard seeds. When they begin to
sputter, add 10 curry leaves and
1 teaspoon curry powder, then crack
in 3 eggs. Baste the eggs with the
ghee and fry for about 2–3 minutes
until the whites are set and the
undersides crisp.

Preheat your oven to 230°C/450°F/gas mark
8. Tip the ghee or butter and the oil from the
mackerel can into a medium-sized roasting
tin. Add the onions and roast for 15 minutes,
stirring from time to time, until golden and
starting to catch in places. Remove from
the oven and stir in the chilli, bay leaf, curry
powder and cardamom pods; then pop back
into the oven for another 10 minutes.

Remove from the oven and stir in the lentils,
rice, measured boiling water and a good pinch
of salt. Cover tightly with foil (this is essential
to make sure the steam stays in and the rice
cooks properly). Reduce the oven temperature
to 220°C/425°F/gas mark 7 and bake for
15 minutes.

Turn off the oven and remove the roasting tin.
Peel back the foil and stir the rice, then lie
the mackerel on top. Replace the foil and pop
back into the oven for 5 minutes to allow the
mackerel to warm in the residual heat. Serve
with a dollop of plain yogurt and some sliced
cucumber and tomatoes, if you fancy.

ALSO WORKS WELL WITH

Hot-smoked salmon fillets, skin discarded

Hot-smoked trout fillets, skin discarded

For both of the above, you may need to use
a little extra ghee to make up for the lack
of canned fish oil

SEAFOOD ORZO
WITH PEPPERS & SAFFRON

This dish is one to pull out for a special occasion. It's such a gorgeous centrepiece but so easy to rustle up. Saffron brings a wonderfully sweet and floral note, but you can do it without — try adding a few strips of orange and lemon zest instead. Serve up with a leafy salad dressed in olive oil and lemon juice.

SERVES 3

2 garlic cloves, crushed

1 rosemary sprig

pinch of chilli flakes

2 tablespoons olive oil

2 red, yellow or orange peppers, cut into smallish chunks

250g (9oz) cherry tomatoes

1 chicken or vegetable stock cube

550ml (19fl oz) boiling water

pinch of saffron

400g (14oz) can plum tomatoes

250g (9oz) orzo pasta

9 shell-on raw prawns

12 live clams, prepared according to the instructions on page 16

zest of 1 unwaxed lemon, plus lemon wedges to serve

sea salt and freshly ground black pepper

grated Parmesan cheese, to serve (optional)

Preheat your oven to 220°C/425°F/gas mark 7. In a medium-sized roasting tin, toss together the garlic, rosemary, chilli flakes, olive oil, peppers and cherry tomatoes. Season, then roast for 15 minutes, tossing from time to time.

Dissolve the stock cube in the measured boiling water, adding the saffron to infuse.

Once the peppers are looking burnished in places, remove the roasting tin from the oven. Add the plum tomatoes, breaking them up a little with a wooden spoon. Then add the infused stock and orzo to the tin and stir to combine. Season again, then cover with foil and pop in the oven for 12 minutes.

Remove from the oven, peel off the foil and give the orzo a good stir: loosen any bits that are sticking at the edges and redistribute. Pop the foil on again and return to the oven for 3 minutes. By now, most of the liquid should be absorbed and the orzo should be al dente.

Remove from the oven and take off the foil. Give the orzo another stir before tucking in the prawns and clams. Bake for a further 3–4 minutes until the prawns turn pink and the clams pop open (discard any that remain closed). Sprinkle over the lemon zest and serve with some lemon wedges. At the risk of being controversial, you might like to grate over a little Parmesan cheese, too.

ALSO WORKS WELL WITH

Swap clams for live mussels

STICKY MISO SALMON
WITH SWEET POTATOES & PEANUT SAUCE

Caramelised sweet potatoes are the perfect companion to the salmon, salty, peanut sauce and sharp pickled ginger. The sauce is delicious, so feel free to double it for an extra saucy experience, or for spooning on to other things later. This dish also works really well at room temperature: flake any leftover salmon and mix with the potatoes, along with some salad leaves and chopped cucumber for a speedy lunch.

SERVES 2

1 tablespoon brown miso paste

2 tablespoons Shaoxing wine

2 teaspoons rice wine vinegar

2 tablespoons runny honey

2 salmon fillets (about 120g/4¼oz each)

2 sweet potatoes, cut into 2.5cm (1in) chunks

2 tablespoons sunflower oil

30g (1oz) pickled sushi ginger, roughly chopped (or 1 teaspoon finely grated fresh root ginger added to the sauce)

4 spring onions, thinly sliced

freshly ground black pepper

FOR THE PEANUT SAUCE

2 tablespoons crunchy peanut butter

1 teaspoon rice wine vinegar

½ tablespoon soy sauce

1 teaspoon sesame oil

1 tablespoon Chinese chilli oil

Preheat your oven to 220°C/425°F/gas mark 7. In a small bowl, mix the miso paste with the Shaoxing wine, rice wine vinegar and honey. Slather this mixture over the salmon and leave to marinate while you cook the sweet potatoes.

In a small roasting tin, toss the sweet potato chunks with the sunflower oil, then season with pepper and pop into the oven for 30 minutes.

Remove the tin from the oven and arrange the salmon fillets on top of the sweet potato chunks. Drizzle the excess marinade over the potatoes and return the tin to the oven for 7–8 minutes until the salmon is just blush in the centre and has a light pink exterior. If you prefer it more well done, leave it in a little longer for a totally cooked-through fillet.

Meanwhile, make the peanut sauce by mixing all the ingredients together in a small bowl or jug. Beat in a little warm water to get it to a drizzling consistency (about 1 tablespoon).

To serve, drizzle the peanut sauce over the contents of the roasting tin and top with the pickled ginger and sliced spring onions.

ALSO WORKS WELL WITH

Mackerel fillets

Trout fillets

Firm white fish fillets, such as pollack, pollock, haddock, tilapia or hake

JAPANESE-STYLE PANCAKE
WITH CORN, CABBAGE & PRAWNS

This is an oven-baked take on the Japanese street food classic okonomiyaki. Play with the fillings: try cooked egg noodles, kimchi, squid, cooked mussels, bacon or scallops. If you can get your mitts on the traditional toppings – bonito flakes and seaweed flakes – use these to top off your baked pancakes, along with the sauce, mayo and pickled ginger in the recipe below.

SERVES 4

200g (7oz) self-raising flour

5 medium eggs

250ml (9fl oz) cooled fish, chicken or dashi stock

3 tablespoons sunflower oil

½ sweetheart cabbage (about 350g/12oz), any tough core removed, shredded

198g (7oz) can sweetcorn, drained

50g (1¾oz) Cheddar cheese

150g (5½oz) raw shelled prawns

4 spring onions, thinly sliced

sea salt and freshly ground black pepper

mayonnaise, to serve

pickled sushi ginger, to serve

FOR THE SAUCE

4 tablespoons tomato ketchup

1 tablespoon Worcestershire sauce

1 tablespoon light soy sauce

2 teaspoons soft brown sugar

Preheat your oven to 200°C/400°F/gas mark 6. Tip the flour into a large bowl and whisk in the eggs, then slowly beat in the stock to create a batter. Season and set aside.

Pour the oil into a medium-sized roasting tin, then tilt the tin carefully to coat all the sides with oil. Pop the roasting tin into the oven to preheat for 7 minutes.

Return to your batter and gently mix in the cabbage, sweetcorn, cheese, prawns and spring onions. Pour the batter into the hot roasting tin, then bake for 25–30 minutes until a skewer poked into the middle comes out clean.

Meanwhile, make your sauce. In a small jug or bowl, combine the ketchup, Worcestershire sauce, soy sauce and sugar, then set aside.

Once your pancake is ready, drizzle over the sauce, dollop on some mayonnaise and sprinkle with some roughly chopped sushi ginger before serving.

ALSO WORKS WELL WITH

Squid rings

Scallops

Precooked mussels

TUNA & TOMATO MACARONI

For me, this book would never have been complete without some sort of tuna pasta bake. This one has an absolute cracker of a topping: chilli, orange and salty pecorino, the perfect balance of spice, sweet and salty savoury. I am a big fan of this old-school staple. I know it's a real divider – I hope you're with me!

SERVES 4

1 large fennel bulb, any tough outer leaves and core discarded, thinly shredded

2 garlic cloves, sliced

2 tablespoons olive oil

350ml (12fl oz) chicken or fish stock

250g (9oz) macaroni pasta

400g (14oz) can cherry tomatoes

400g (14oz) can chopped tomatoes

2 x 160g (5¾oz) cans tuna in olive oil, drained

25g (1oz) pecorino cheese, finely grated

6 tablespoons dried breadcrumbs (such as panko)

zest of ½ unwaxed orange

zest of ½ unwaxed lemon, plus lemon wedges to serve

½ teaspoon pul biber (Aleppo chilli flakes)

sea salt and freshly ground black pepper

Preheat your oven to 220°C/425°F/gas mark 7. In a medium-sized roasting tin, toss the fennel and garlic with the olive oil and 2 tablespoons of water, then season. Pop the dish into the oven for about 10 minutes, stirring now and then until the fennel is soft and turning golden.

Tip the stock into the roasting tin along with the pasta, both types of tomatoes and tuna. Season and cover with foil. Bake for 10 minutes.

Meanwhile, in a small bowl, mix together the pecorino, breadcrumbs, orange and lemon zest and pul biber.

Remove the roasting tin from the oven and take off the foil. Give the pasta a good stir, then sprinkle the breadcrumb mixture over the top. Pop it back into the oven for another 10 minutes until golden. Serve with lemon wedges for squeezing over the top.

ALSO WORKS WELL WITH

Raw or cooked prawns

Tinned mackerel, drained

Crab meat

FISH STEW
WITH CHORIZO, BAY & TOMATOES

This cosy oven-baked stew is perfect for chilly evenings. When I was growing up, my mum often made a chorizo and potato stew that always felt so nourishing and warming. I've added a little chorizo to this fish stew, bringing a wonderfully smoky richness to a gorgeously autumnal dish.

SERVES 2

70g (2½oz) cooking chorizo, cut into very small chunks

2 small onions, thinly sliced

2 garlic cloves, sliced

1 fresh bay leaf

1 rosemary sprig

pinch of chilli flakes

1 celery stick, thinly sliced

4 tablespoons olive oil

150ml (5fl oz) vermouth (I use Noilly Prat)

1 fish stock cube, diluted with 600ml (20fl oz) boiling water

450g (1lb) tomatoes, deseeded and roughly chopped

200g (7oz) potatoes, peeled and cut into little chunks (about 2.5cm/1in)

300g (10½oz) cod loin, skinned and cut into 5cm (2in) chunks

200g (7oz) live mussels, prepared according to the instructions on page 16

sea salt and freshly ground black pepper

lemon wedges, to serve

TIP If you want to make this pescatarian, add a little extra oil and a pinch of sweet paprika at the start of the recipe, along with a few chopped canned anchovies for salty savouriness.

Preheat your oven to 220°C/425°F/gas mark 7. In a medium-sized roasting tin, toss together the chorizo, onions, garlic, bay, rosemary, chilli flakes, celery and olive oil. Pop into the oven for about 10–15 minutes until the onions and celery are tender and turning golden.

Remove the roasting tin from the oven and pour in the vermouth and fish stock. Stir through the tomatoes, then season and return to the oven for 5 minutes.

Remove the tin from the oven and stir in the potatoes. Return to the oven for about 15 minutes until the potatoes are just tender to the point of a knife.

Remove the tin from the oven once more and tuck the fish and mussels into the stew. Return to the oven for a final 5–6 minutes until the fish is opaque and the mussels pop open (discard any that remain closed). Serve with the lemon wedges.

ALSO WORKS WELL WITH

Swap the live mussels for clams

Firm white fish fillets, such as pollack, pollock, haddock, monkfish or hake

HERB-CRUMBED HADDOCK
WITH CHEAT'S RATATOUILLE

Oven-cooking is my favoured method of making ratatouille. You get a gorgeously golden, sticky and soft tangle of summer veg without having to stand over a hob for a prolonged period of time. I haven't included aubergine in this version, but you can add one in place of a courgette.

SERVES 4

2 red peppers, cut into small chunks

6 tablespoons olive oil

3 garlic cloves, 2 sliced and 1 crushed

3 courgettes, cut into small chunks

400g (14oz) small tomatoes

4 slices of bread, crumbled into small pieces (or about 100g/3½oz fresh breadcrumbs)

zest of 1 unwaxed lemon, plus lemon wedges to serve

small handful fresh basil, leaves chopped

small handful fresh flat-leaf parsley, leaves chopped

4 skinless haddock fillets (about 120g/4¼oz each)

sea salt and freshly ground black pepper

Dijon mustard, to serve

Preheat your oven to 240°C/475°F/gas mark 9. In a medium-sized roasting tin, toss together the peppers, 4 tablespoons of the olive oil, the sliced garlic cloves and the courgettes. Season and pop into the oven for 15 minutes, shaking halfway through, until the vegetables are starting to look burnished.

Remove the roasting tin from the oven and add the tomatoes, then pop back into the oven for 15 minutes.

Meanwhile, to make the herb crust, mix together the remaining oil and the crushed garlic with the breadcrumbs, lemon zest and herbs.

Remove the roasting tin from the oven once again and place the fish fillets on top of the ratatouille. Create a crust over each by scattering over the herby breadcrumbs. Reduce the oven temperature to 210°C/410°F/gas mark 6 and bake for about 8 minutes until the fish is opaque and flakes easily. Serve with some lemon wedges and a little dollop of mustard on the side.

ALSO WORKS WELL WITH

Firm white fish fillets, such as pollack, pollock, haddock, tilapia or hake

Salmon fillets

Trout fillets

WHOLE SEA BREAM ON TANGY AUBERGINE & CELERY

The sticky, sweet and sharp vegetables under the sea bream here are wonderful in many incarnations. They are ideal for batch cooking and delicious served on toast, with a perky roast chicken, folded into a frittata or as a side for grilled tuna.

SERVES 2

2 small aubergines, cut into small chunks, roughly 3cm (1¼in)

1 large red onion, chopped

2 celery sticks, chopped into small pieces, roughly 2cm (¾in)

2 garlic cloves, sliced

6 tablespoons olive oil, plus extra to drizzle

2 x 400g (14oz) cans plum tomatoes, drained

1½ tablespoons red wine vinegar

1 teaspoon caster sugar

2 tablespoons capers

1 tablespoon sultanas

1 whole sea bream (about 700g/1lb 9oz), scaled and gutted

½ lemon, sliced

small handful of fresh basil leaves, roughly torn

sea salt and freshly ground black pepper

Preheat your oven to 220°C/425°F/gas mark 7. In a large roasting tin, toss the aubergines, onion, celery and garlic with the olive oil. Season, then roast for 15 minutes, stirring from time to time, until tender and starting to colour.

Remove the roasting tin from the oven and add the tomatoes, breaking them up as you stir them in. Return to the oven for another 10 minutes.

Remove the roasting tin from the oven once again and stir in the vinegar, sugar, capers and sultanas. Lie the fish on top and stuff the fish cavity with the lemon slices. Season the sea bream inside and out with salt and black pepper, then drizzle with oil. Roast for 15–20 minutes until the flesh is opaque and comes away from the bone easily. Gently stir the basil into the tangy vegetable and serve.

ALSO WORKS WELL WITH
Whole sea bass

Whole trout

Whole gurnard

INDEX

ABOUT THE AUTHOR

Lola's eyes were opened to the world of cookbooks, food photography and styling when she did work experience with Jamie Oliver and his food team. After school, she went to Glasgow School of Art and studied Fine Art Photography, though food continued to weave through her work there. After graduating she decided to return to the world of food styling and started working in the kitchens of cafés and bakeries while doing work experience with food stylists. She then progressed to assisting full time and then to being a stylist herself, expanding along the way into recipe testing and then writing. Lola's first book, *Take One Tin*, was published by Kyle Books in 2020 and selected as one of the *Independent*'s ten best store cupboard cookbooks.

US GLOSSARY

allotment – community garden
aubergine – eggplant
beetroot – beet
broad bean – fava bean
butter bean – lima bean
caster sugar – superfine sugar
chicory – endive
chickpeas – garbanzo beans
coriander – cilantro
cornichons – baby pickles
courgette – zucchini
crème fraîche – sour cream
double cream – heavy cream
flaked almonds – slivered almonds
King Edward potato – round white or red potato
kipper – smoked herring
monkfish – angler fish
pepper, red/green/yellow – bell pepper
petit pois – petite sweet peas
plain flour – all-purpose flour
(king) prawns – (jumbo) shrimp
self-raising flour – self-rising flour
soft brown sugar – brown sugar
soured cream – sour cream
spring onion – scallion
streaky bacon – bacon
sultana – golden raisin
sweetcorn – corn
tomato purée – tomato paste
turnip – rutabaga

Picture credits:
14–15 Kristin Snippe/Unsplash
54–5 Dan Richards/iStock
80–1 kodachrome25/iStock
102–3 omnimarketing/iStock
130–1 cstewart/iStock
154–5 David Clode/Unsplash

An Hachette UK Company
www.hachette.co.uk

First published in Great Britain in 2021 by
Kyle Books, an imprint of
Octopus Publishing Group Limited
Carmelite House
50 Victoria Embankment
London EC4Y 0DZ
www.kylebooks.co.uk
www.octopusbooksusa.com

ISBN: 9780857839480

Text copyright 2021 © Lola Milne
Design and layout copyright 2021 © Octopus
Publishing Group Limited
Photography copyright 2021 © Lizzie Mayson

Distributed in the US by Hachette Book Group,
1290 Avenue of the Americas, 4th and 5th Floors,
New York, NY 10104

Distributed in Canada by Canadian Manda Group,
664 Annette St., Toronto, Ontario, Canada M6S 2C8

Lola Milne is hereby identified as the author of this
work in accordance with Section 77 of the Copyright,
Designs and Patents Act 1988

All rights reserved. No part of this work may be
reproduced or utilised in any form or by any means,
electronic or mechanical, including photocopying,
recording or by any information storage and retrieval
system, without the prior written permission of
the publisher.

Editorial Director: Judith Hannam
Publisher: Joanna Copestick
Editor: Florence Filose
Design: Louise Leffler
Photography: Lizzie Mayson
Food styling: Lola Milne
Prop styling: Louie Waller
Illustration: Marie Doazan
Production: Allison Gonsalves

A Cataloguing in Publication record for this title
is available from the British Library

Printed and bound in China

10 9 8 7 6 5 4 3 2 1

THANK YOU

A BOOK IS THE WORK OF MANY. THANK YOU, THANK YOU TO LIZZIE, LOUIE, SOPHIE, INDIA, FLORENCE, JUDITH, LOUISE AND MARIE. GIANT THANK YOUS TO LUKE AND CIARA, TAZI, AJIA AND SAM, RACHEL, SIOBHAN, FAYE, CONNIE AND MAX, ANNA AND PAOLO, ELLA, STARZY AND JOE, MILLY, ELLA AND MARTIN, JASMINE, RIO, INDIA, JOHN & ALICE, AGATA, KAT, SOPHIE, JAYNEY, HANNAH, IMOGEN, ELLA, EVE AND BEATRIX. LAST BUT ABSOLUTELY NOT LEAST, NEVER ENDING THANK YOUS, MUM, DAD, MY BROTHER BRODIE, KENDALL AND TO MY DEAREST, JAMIE.